13 Ways of Looking at a Blackbird

2002-2012

Holly Crawford

Lokke
New York

Daria Hollowell, C. Wil Hollowell, Francis Hollowell, Carles Albert Casanova, Bill Shissler, Peter Frank, James Knowles, Matthew Semler, Felix Lazo, Maria Angelica Lapostol Luco & George Crawford. Thank you!

www.art-poetry.info

ISBN: 978-0-9852461-74

" 'Thirteen Ways of Looking at a Blackbird' is a way of declaring that no blackbird exists and that instead there are only varieties of imaginary perspective that may bring blackbirds into being." Harold Rosenburg, *The Anxious Object*

Creation and destruction, time and change, impermanence, indeterminacy, the ordinary. We need to invest energy to make something we want come together. This project is relational and situational.

"Things fall apart. Get used to it." Yeats

Sculptural forms and entire environments are created from air and black latex balloons. The black latex balloons differ in size and shapes. Latex is a natural material that decomposes in about the same time as a banana skin when light and water contact it.

Dali once quipped, "that the least one can ask of a piece of sculpture is not to move…."

The balloons have a predetermined shape, but are still unique. The balloons are like cells that come together into different spaces. They are connected for a short time.   When massed each sculpture is unique and different every time.

The skin of each balloon changes over time, as does the mass.
Temperature and movements of air will affect each balloon and the mass.
This sculpture is not permanent.

I am not permanent.

" The blackbird is the only element in nature which is aesthetically compatible with bleak light and bare limbs: he is, we may say, a certain kind of language, opposed to euphony, to those "noble accents and lucid inescapable rhythms" which Stevens used so memorably elsewhere in *Harmonium*. … There are thirteen ways of looking at a blackbird because thirteen is the eccentric number; Stevens is almost medieval in his relish for external form. This poetry will be one of inflection and innuendo; the inflections are the heard melodies (the whistling of the blackbird) and the innuendoes are what is left out (the silence just after the whistling) …

… The blackbird has perhaps something in common with Eliot's "shadow" that falls between potency and act, desire and consummation [in "The Hollow Men"]. But Stevens would deny that it is remediable or accidental intrusion between two things that without it would be better off. It is, rather, of one substance with the things it relates:

I do not know which to prefer,
The beauty of inflections
Or the beauty of innuendoes,
The blackbird whistling
Or just after. (iv)

Between the man and the woman is the blackbird, one with them; between the man's mood and his environment is the blackbird, the indecipherable cause of the mood which is man's response to nature (stanza vi); between the man of Haddam and their imagined golden birds is the blackbird, the real on which they construct their "artifice of eternity" (vii); between the haunted man and his protective glass coach is the terror of the blackbird (xi); it lies at the base of even our powerful verbal defenses, those beautiful glass coaches of euphony and lucidity/ It is, finally, the principle of our final relation to the universe, our compulsions, first of all,

The river is moving.
The blackbird must be flying. (xii)

and, lastly, our despair at death:
It was evening all afternoon.
It was snowing
And it was going to snow.
The blackbird sat
In the cedar limbs. (xiii)

But neurosis and death are only instances of a pervasive relational eccentricity. Our extent in space (as well as in time) goes only as far as the blackbird goes – the blackbird *is* our "line of vision" (ix), as it is our line of thought: when we are of two minds (or, as Stevens presses it, "of three minds"), it is not as if we had a blackbird, an oriole, and a pigeon in view, but only "a tree / In which there are three blackbirds" (ii). The blackbird is by no means all – it is surrounded by the vastness of twenty mountains, the autumn winds, the snow – but though only a small part, it is the determining focus of relation." Helen Vendler, *On Extended Wings: Wallace Stevens; Longer Poems* (Cambridge: Harvard U P, 1969), 75-77.

Each installation is unique. I construct the temporary sculpture on site from black latex balloons. The black latex balloons differ in size and shapes. For instance, standard rounds are readily available in sizes from 5" to 36" and elongated from 2"x 60" to 7"x 60". Different balloons are massed together and then popped at one moment at the end. Starting with the Riverside Art Museum, they were popped twice. The shards were left and new ones constructed around them. All the airlines were very helpful. Air France was wonderful. I received VIP status. I arrived at airline counters with a very small black bag filled with 2,000 black balloons, fish string and a small inflator. Each time I wondered if the bag would arrive. The first time, in Florence, I took hand pumps. They melted. Really. A compressor was fashioned. My hands were bleeding from tying the balloons. I then figured out how to tie thousands of balloons.

This is the documentation of the first ten years of this project. It was installed in seven different places in the world. It is an installation, participation, performance, and sculpture. Since 2002, it has been installed in Florence, Berlin, and Valencia, London, Riverside, NYC and Chile. It has been installed from 24 hours to 6 weeks. The forms will last for 6 months or more. I would like to thank everyone for their help.

Holly Crawford, New York   March 16, 2013

Florence, Italy

U. S. Consulate Art Gallery, 2002

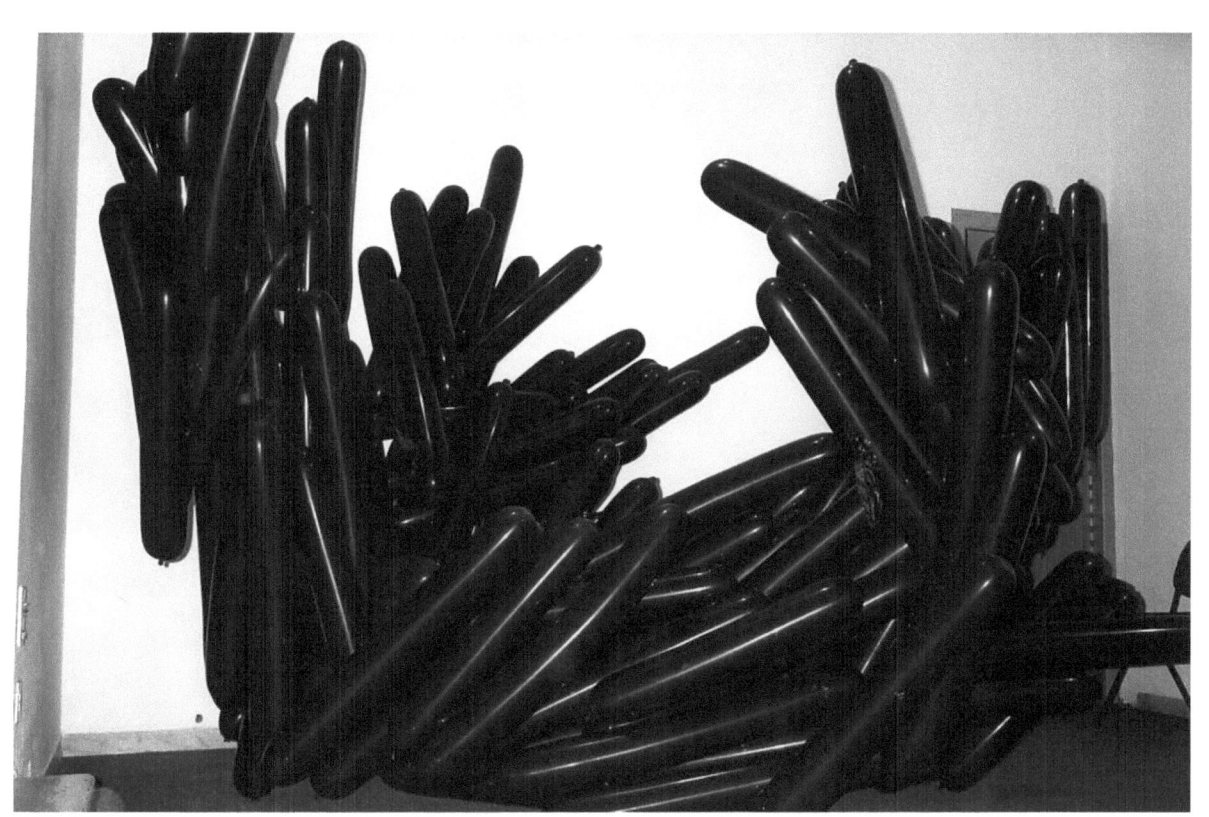

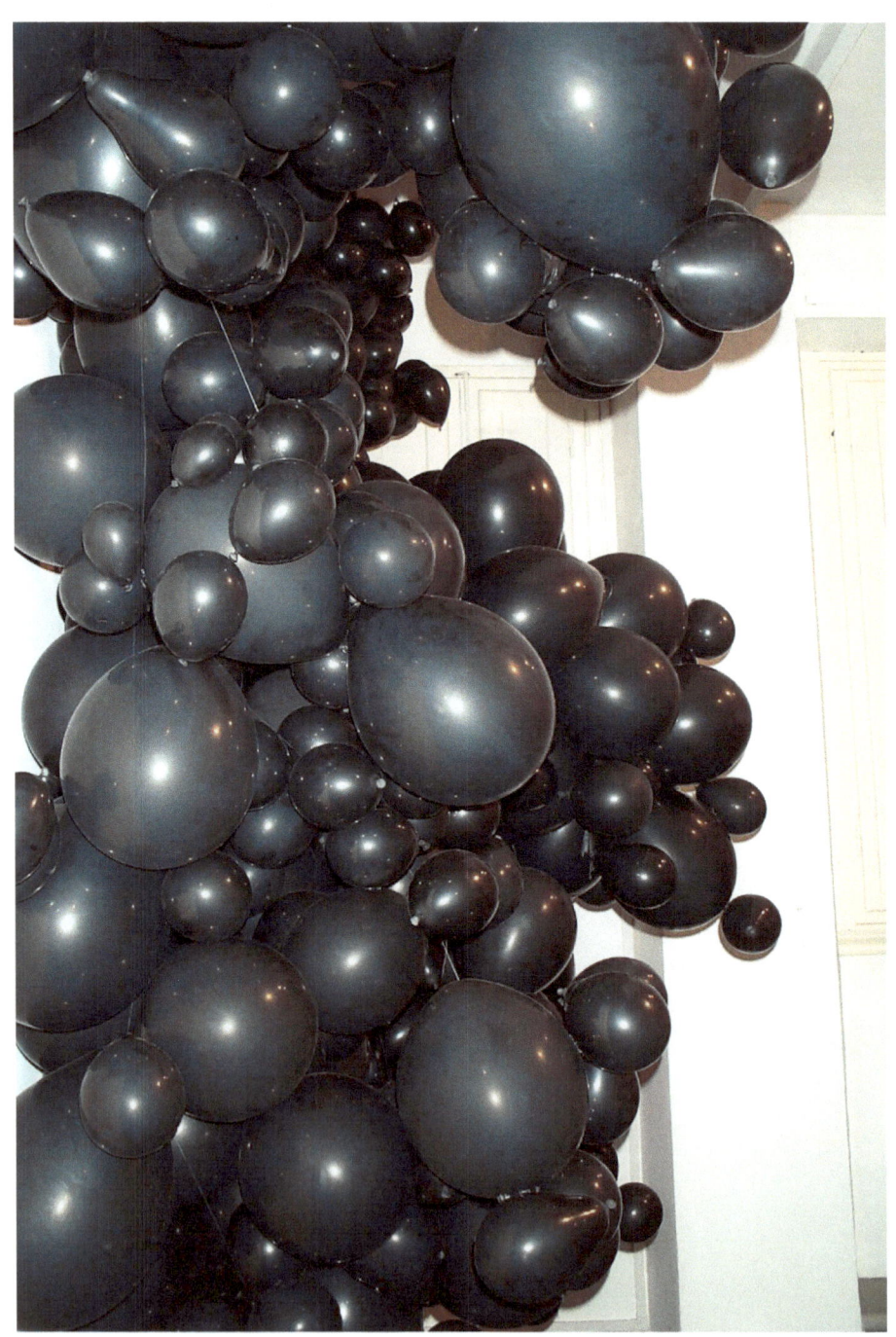

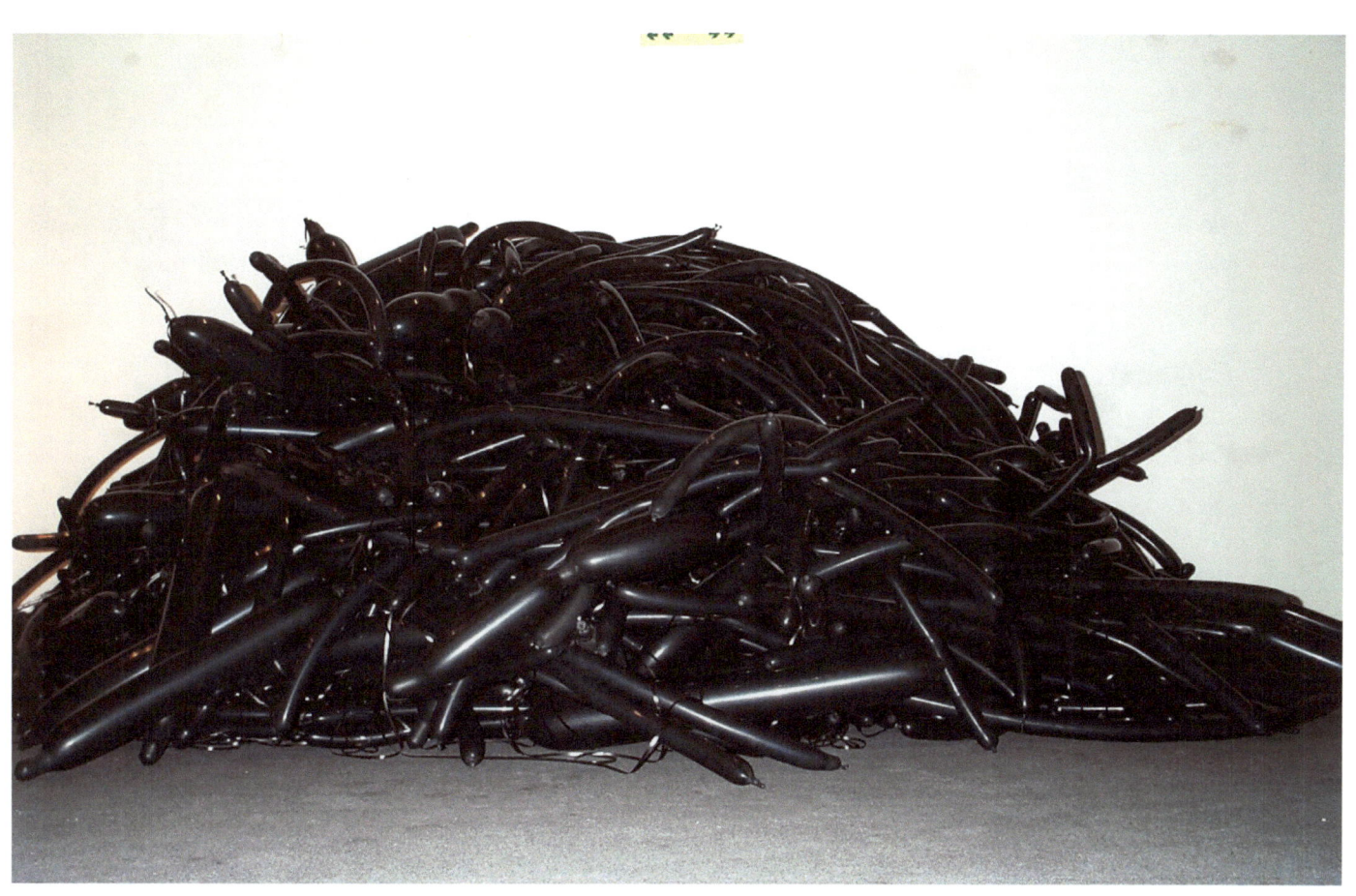

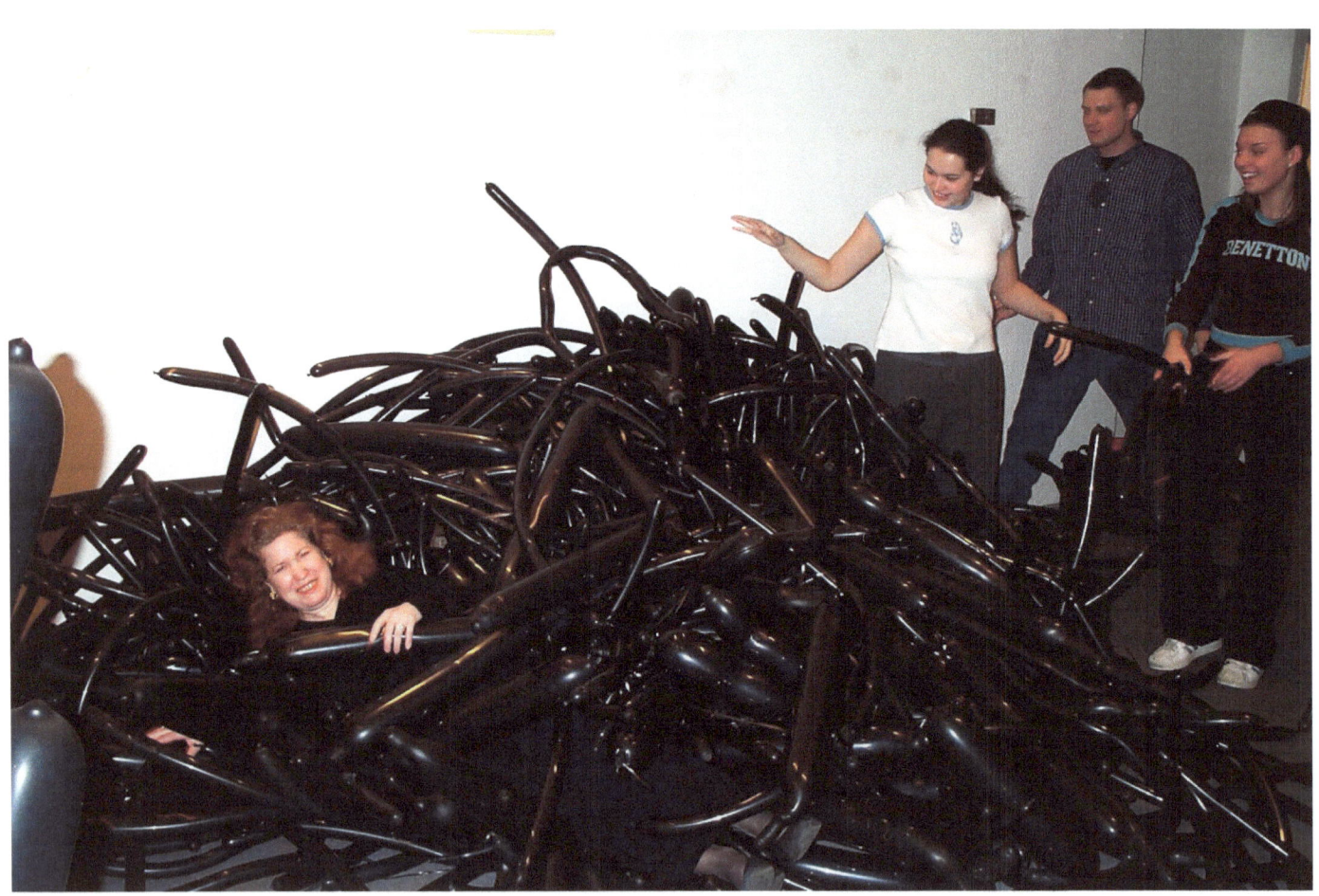

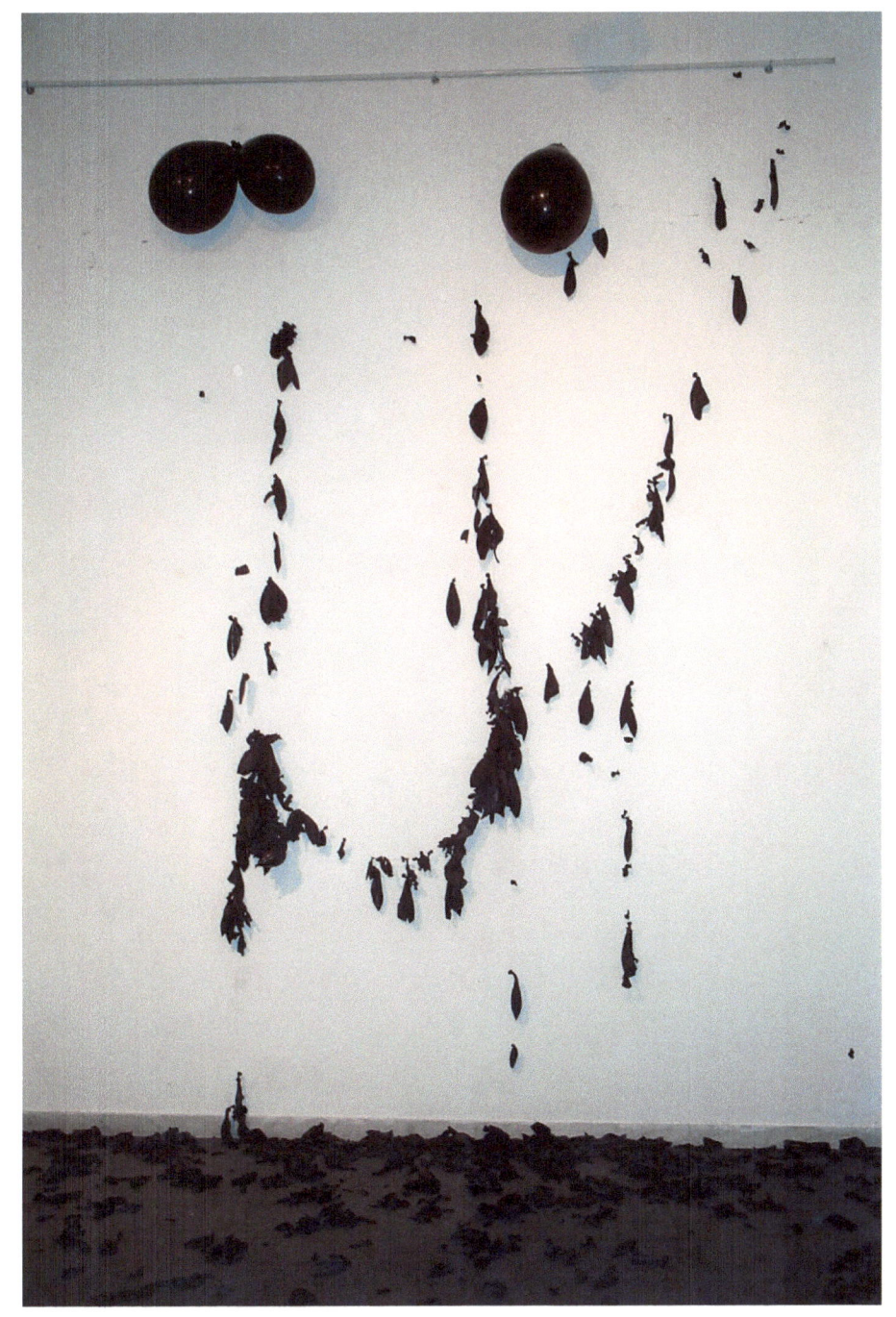

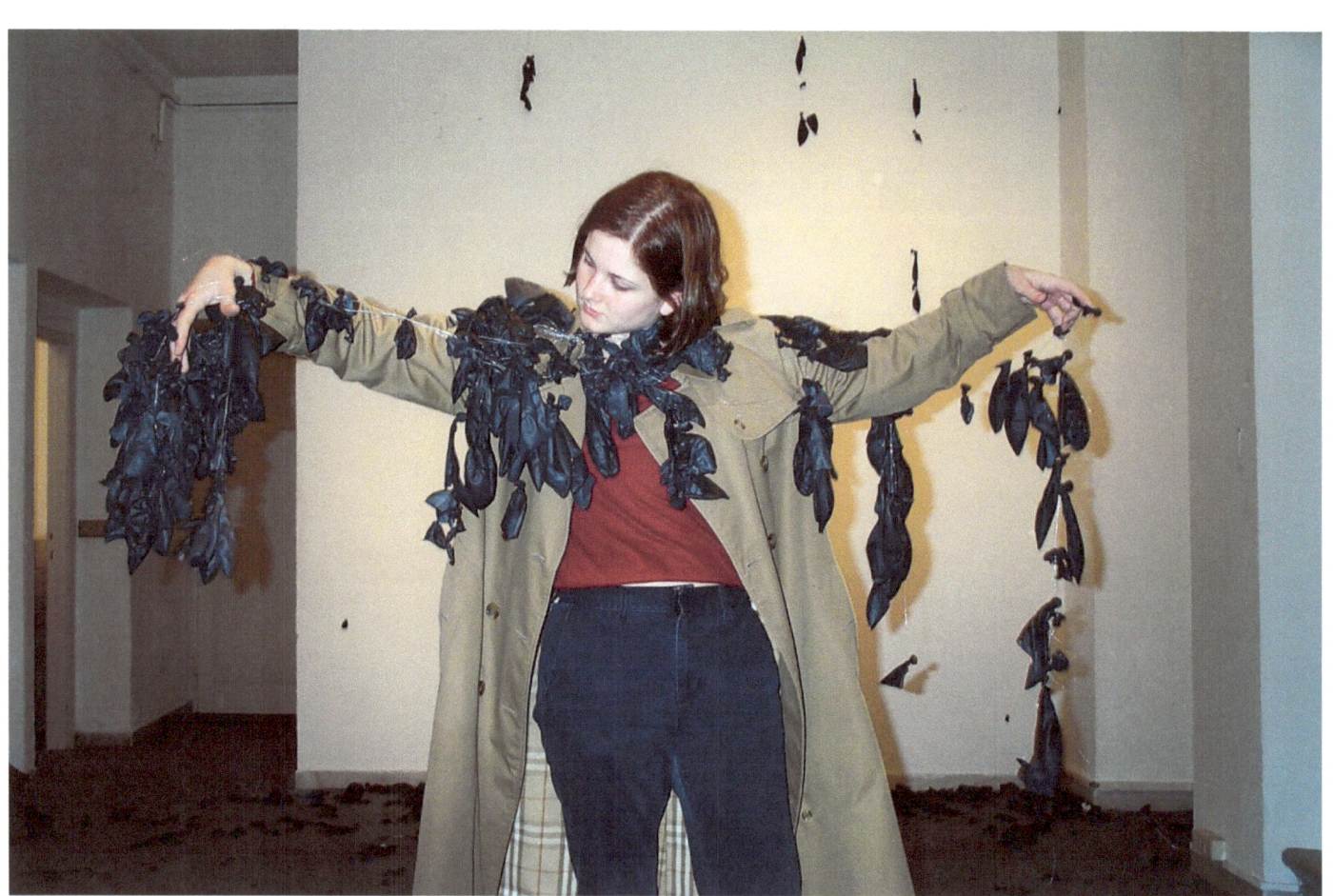

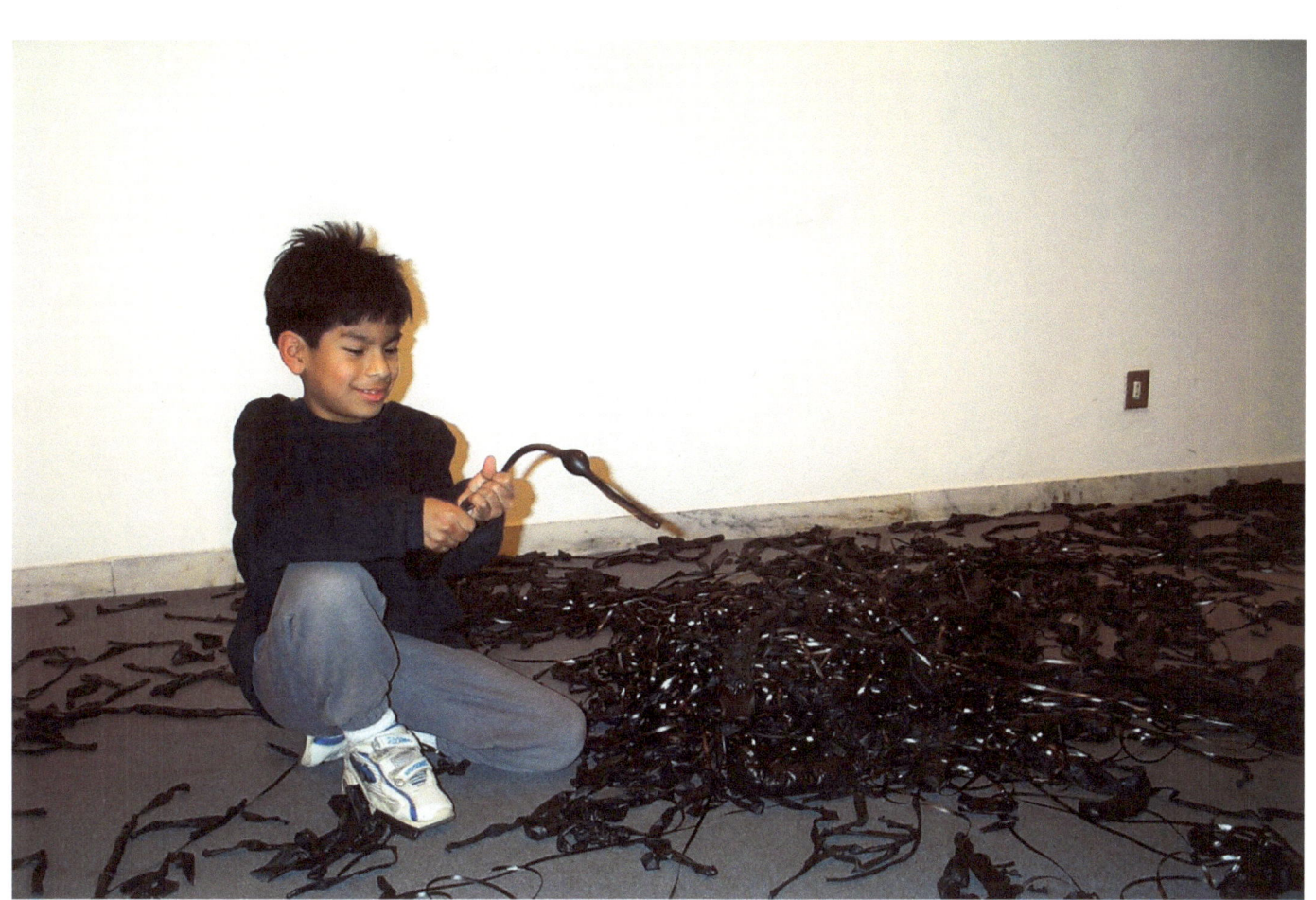

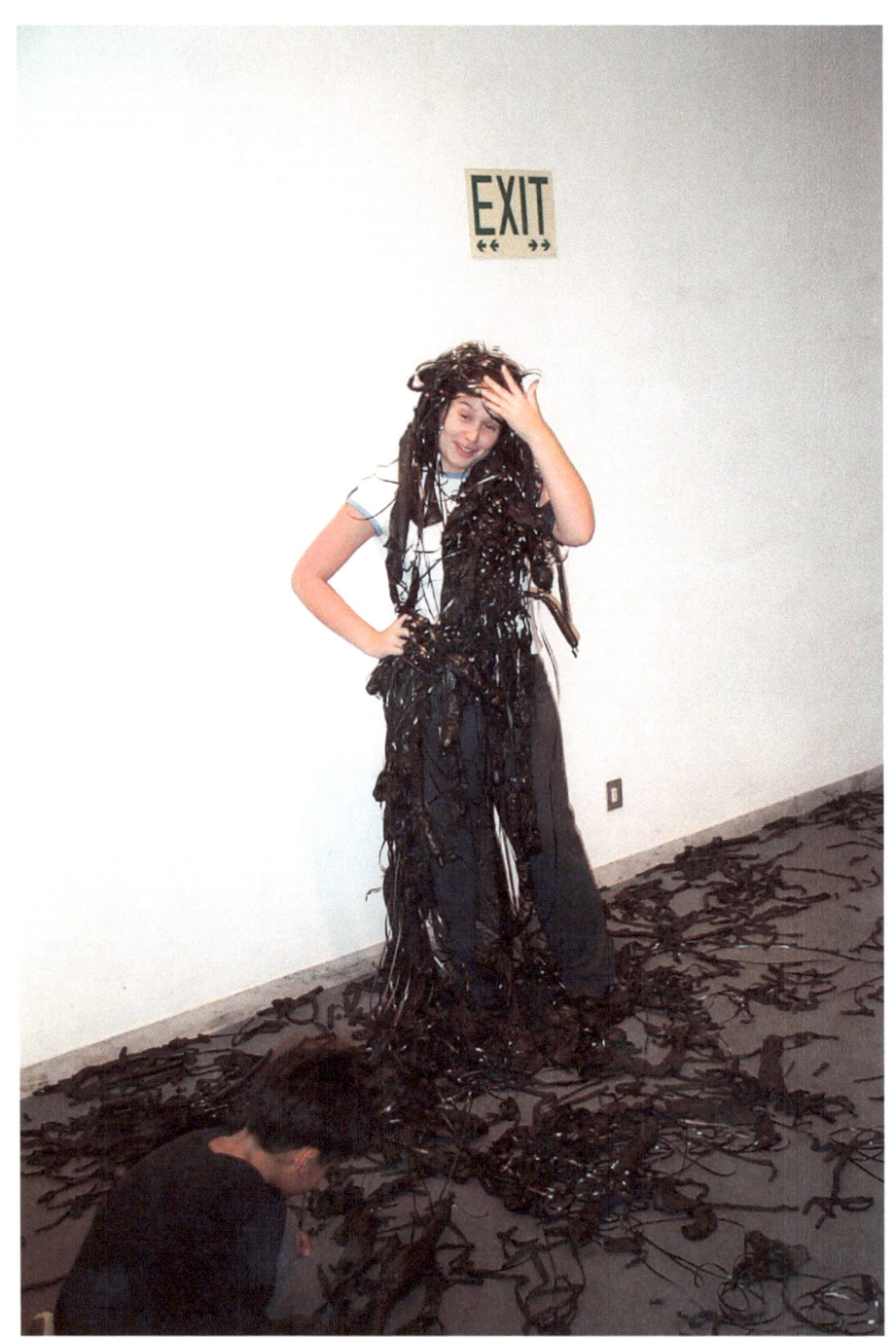

Berlin

Berliner Kunst Gallery, 2004

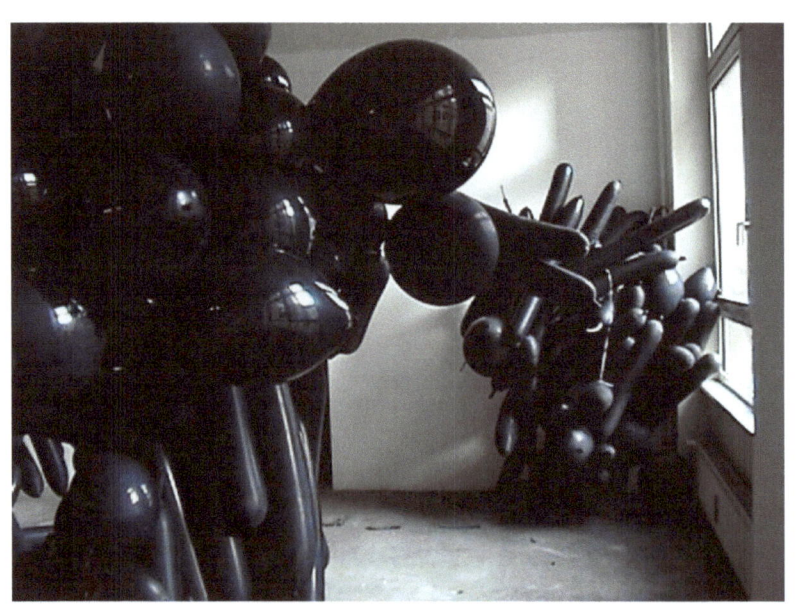

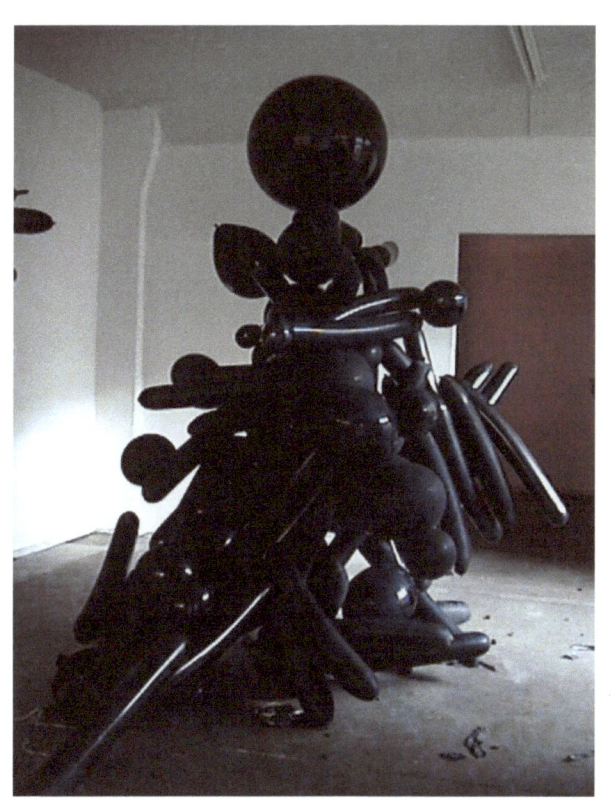

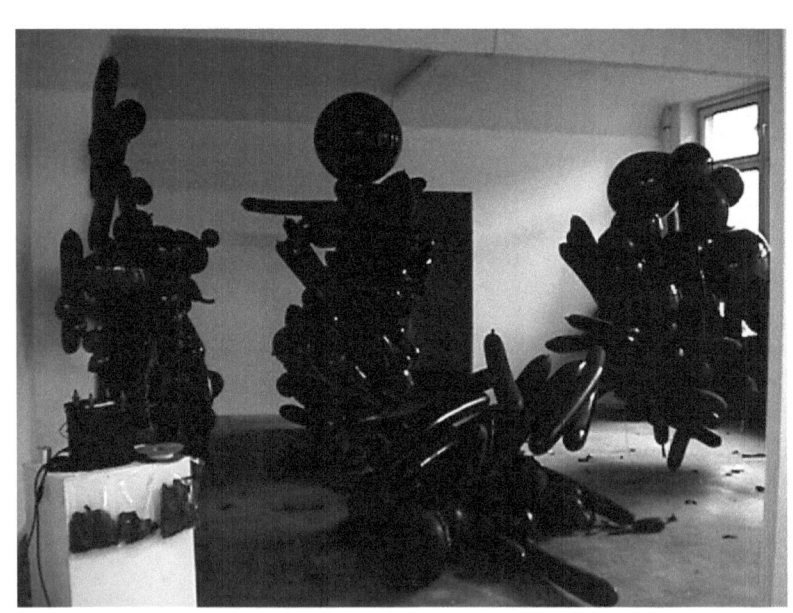

Valencia, Spain

Colorelefante Gallery, 2005

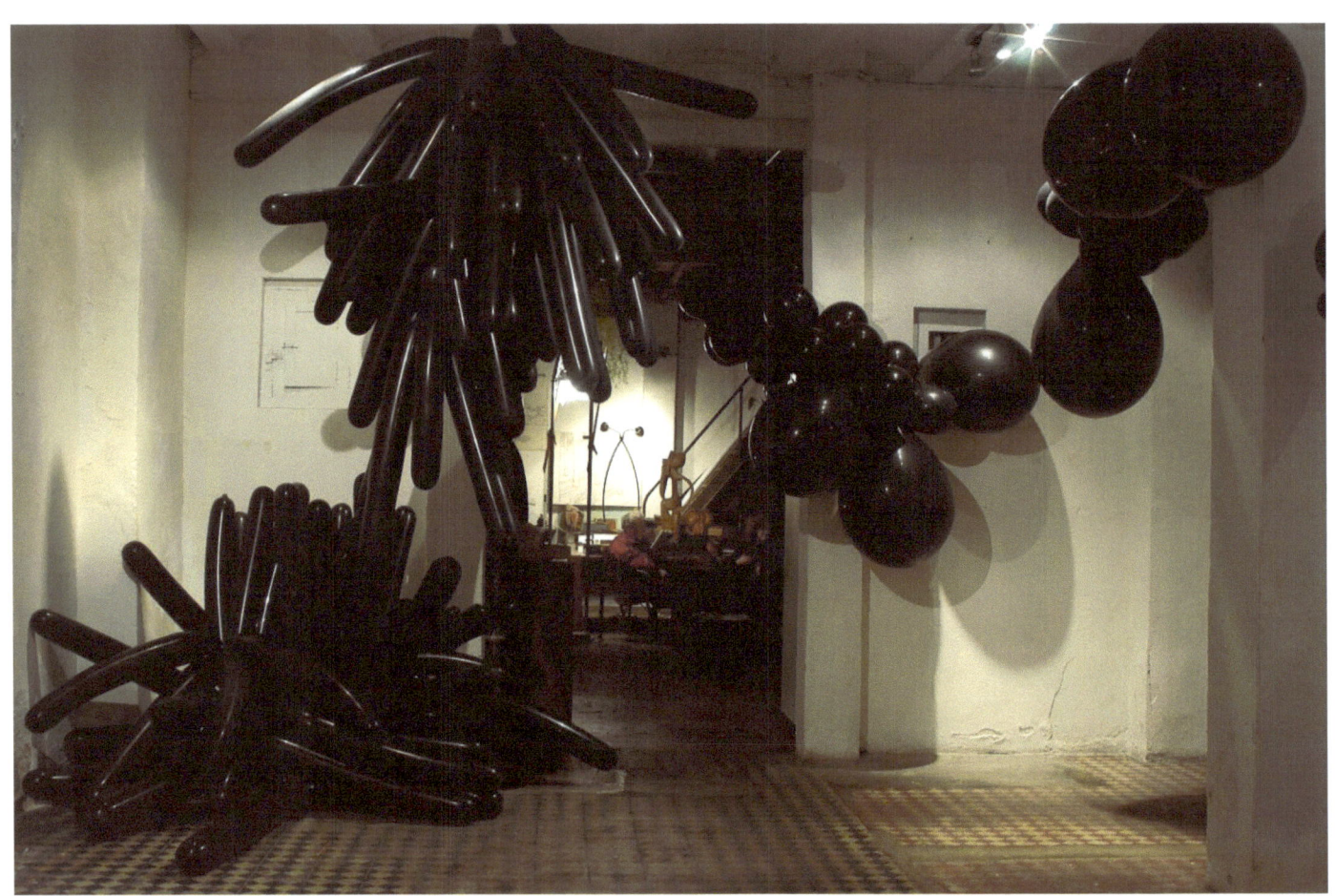

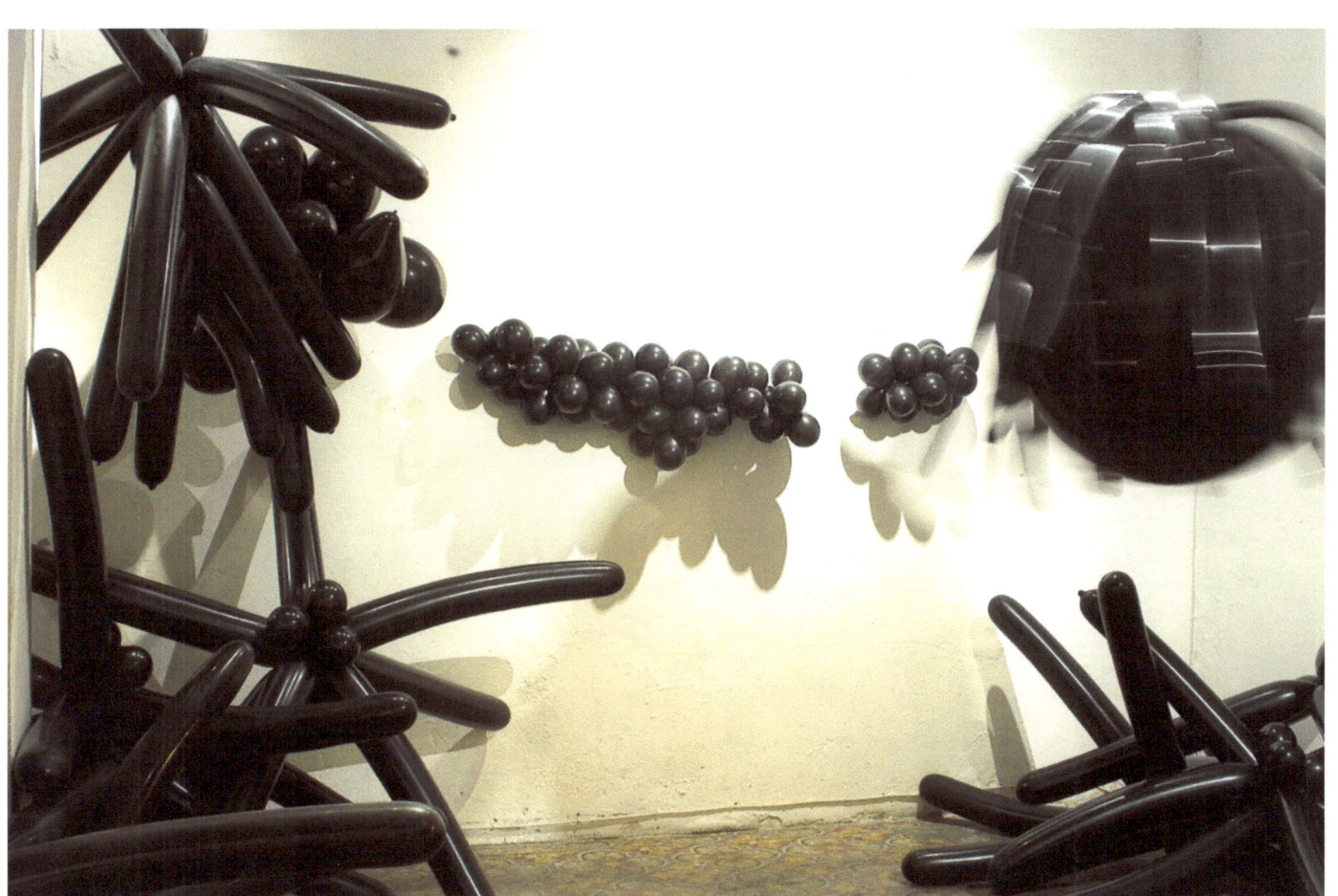

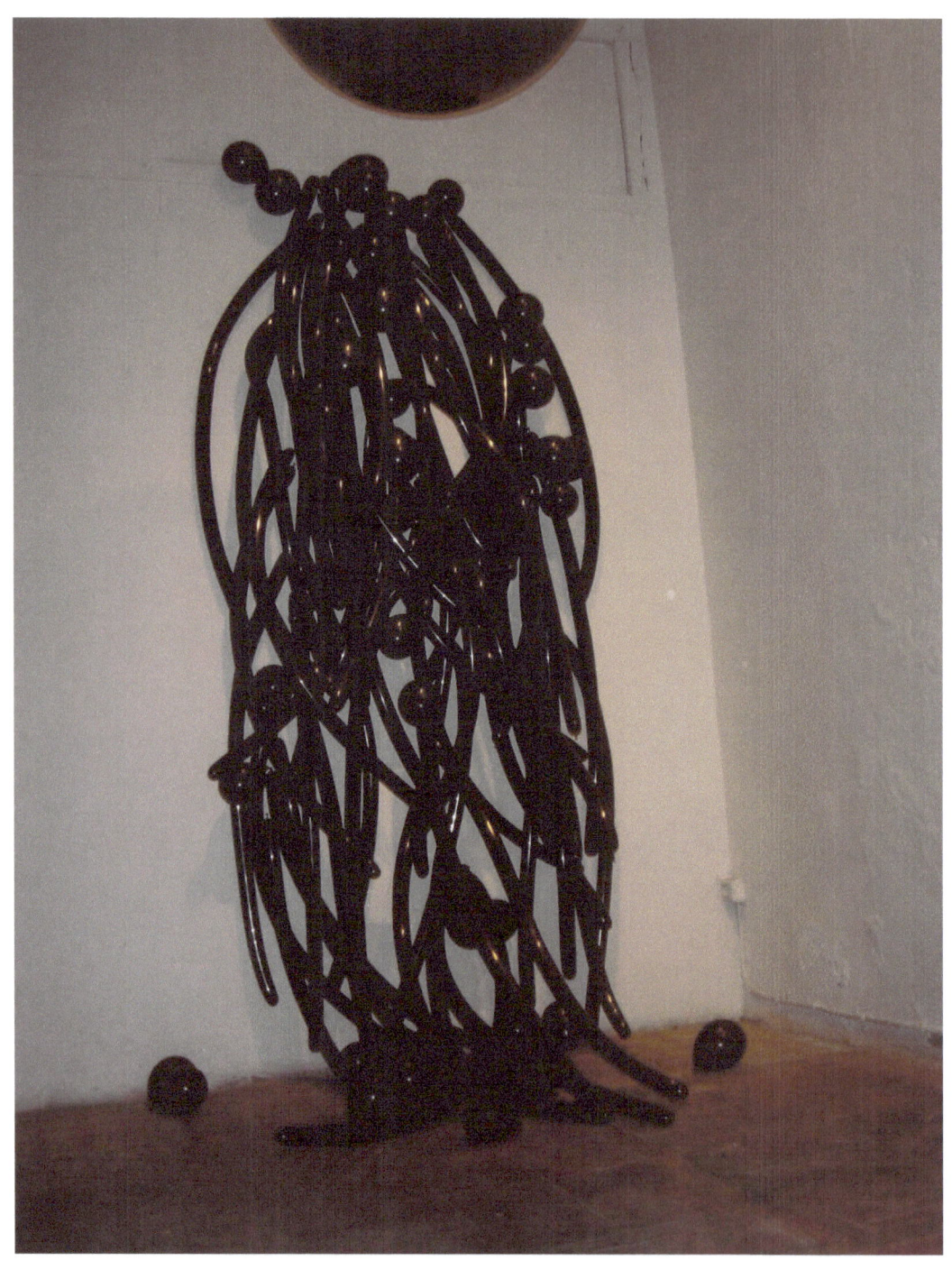

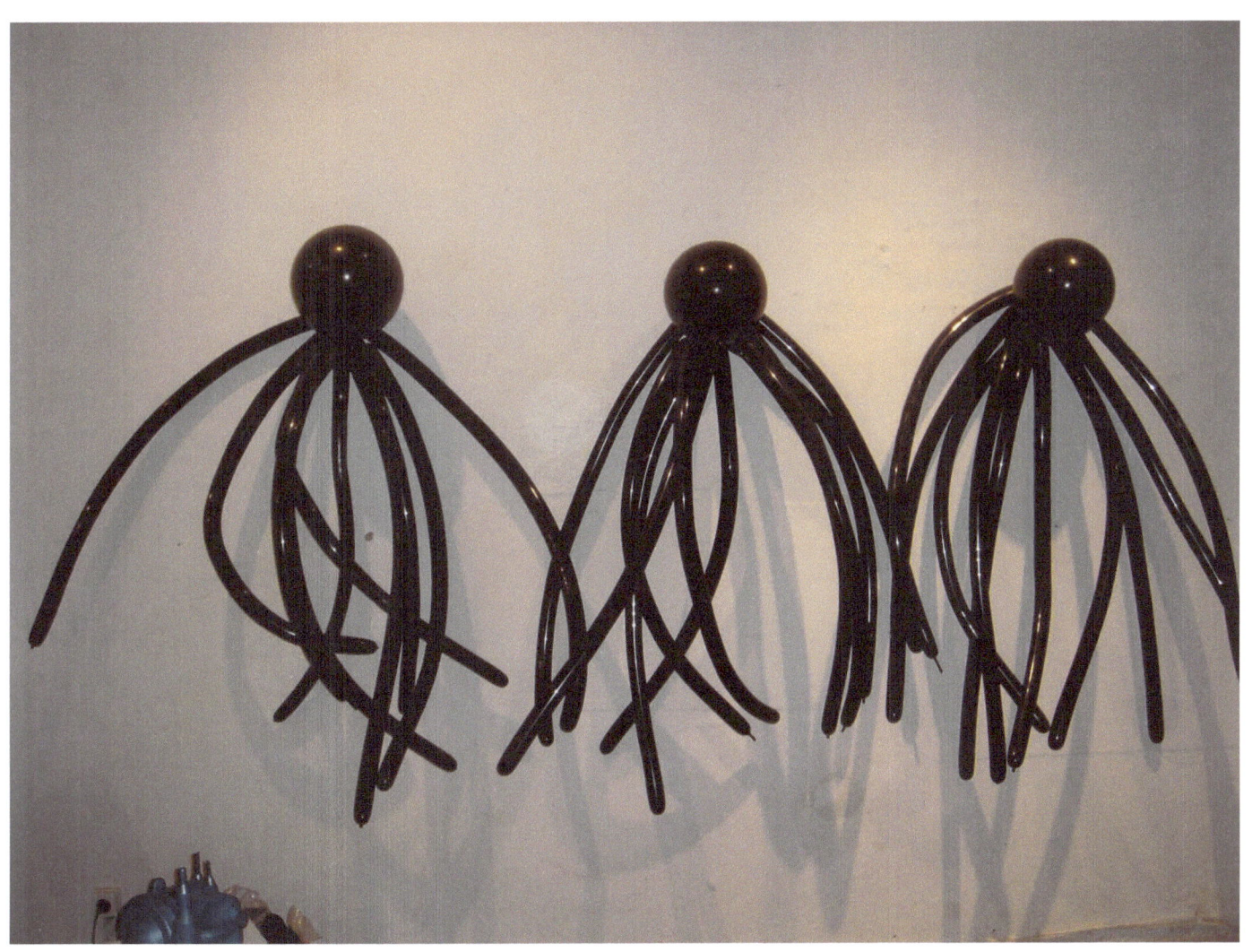

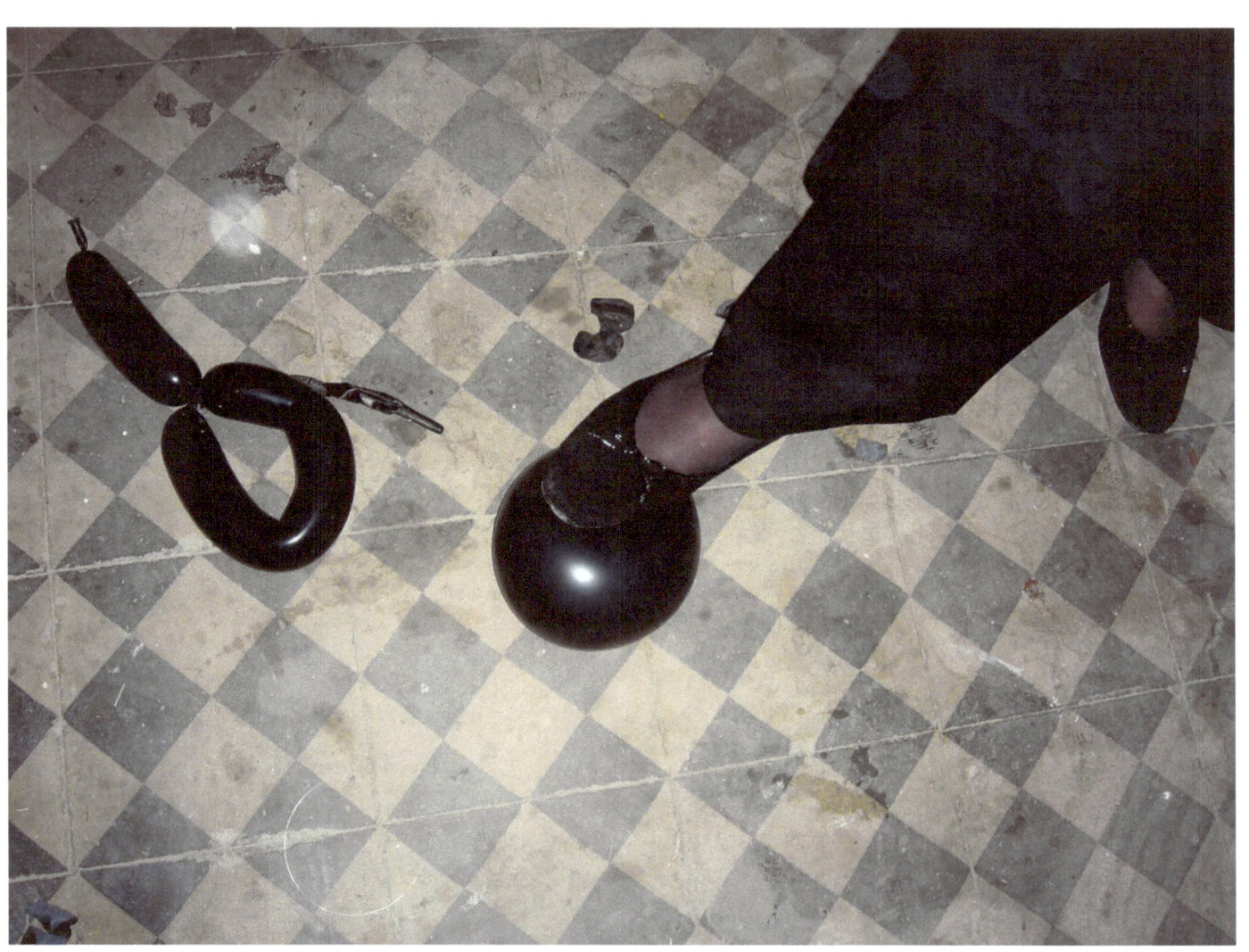

London

SeOne, 2006

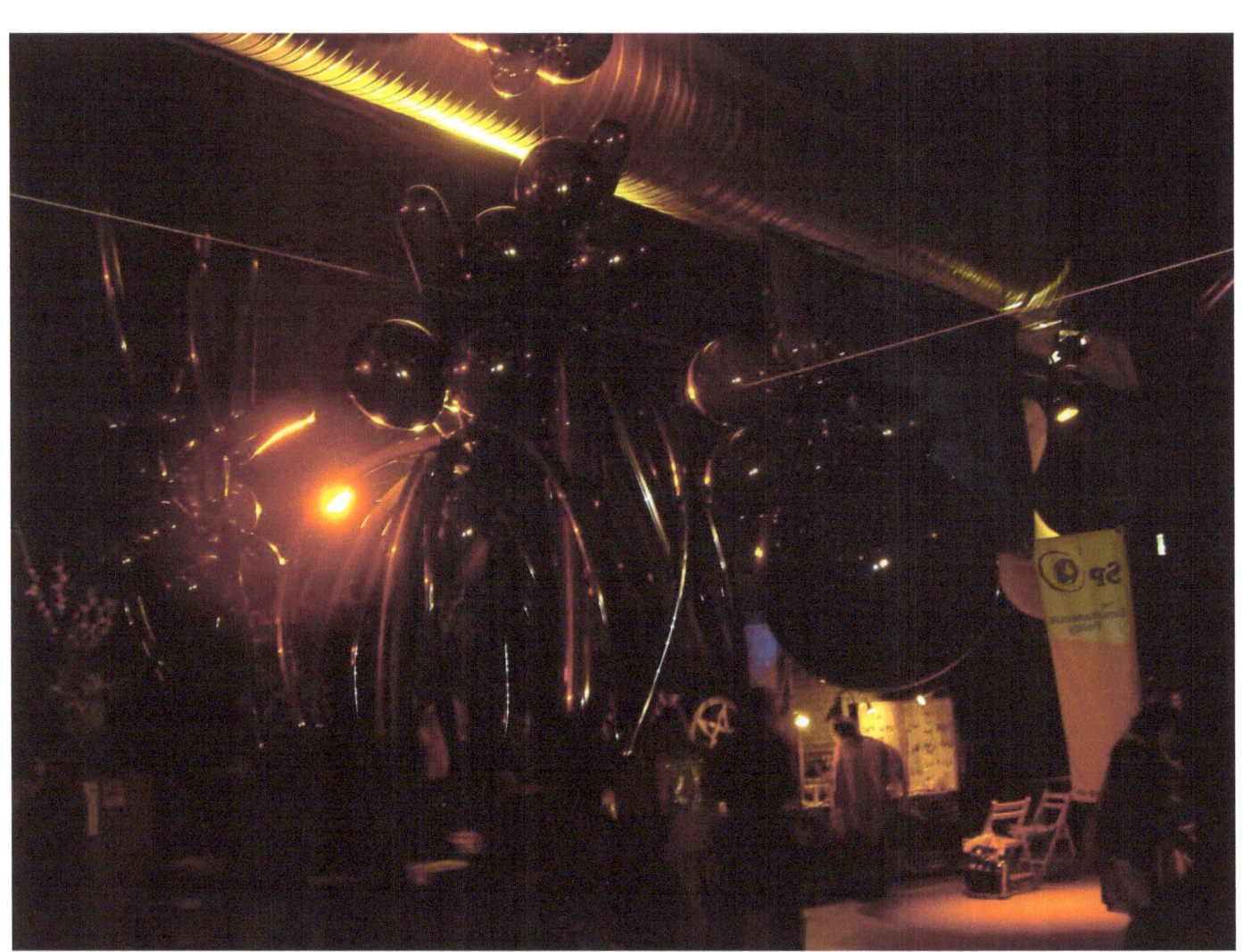

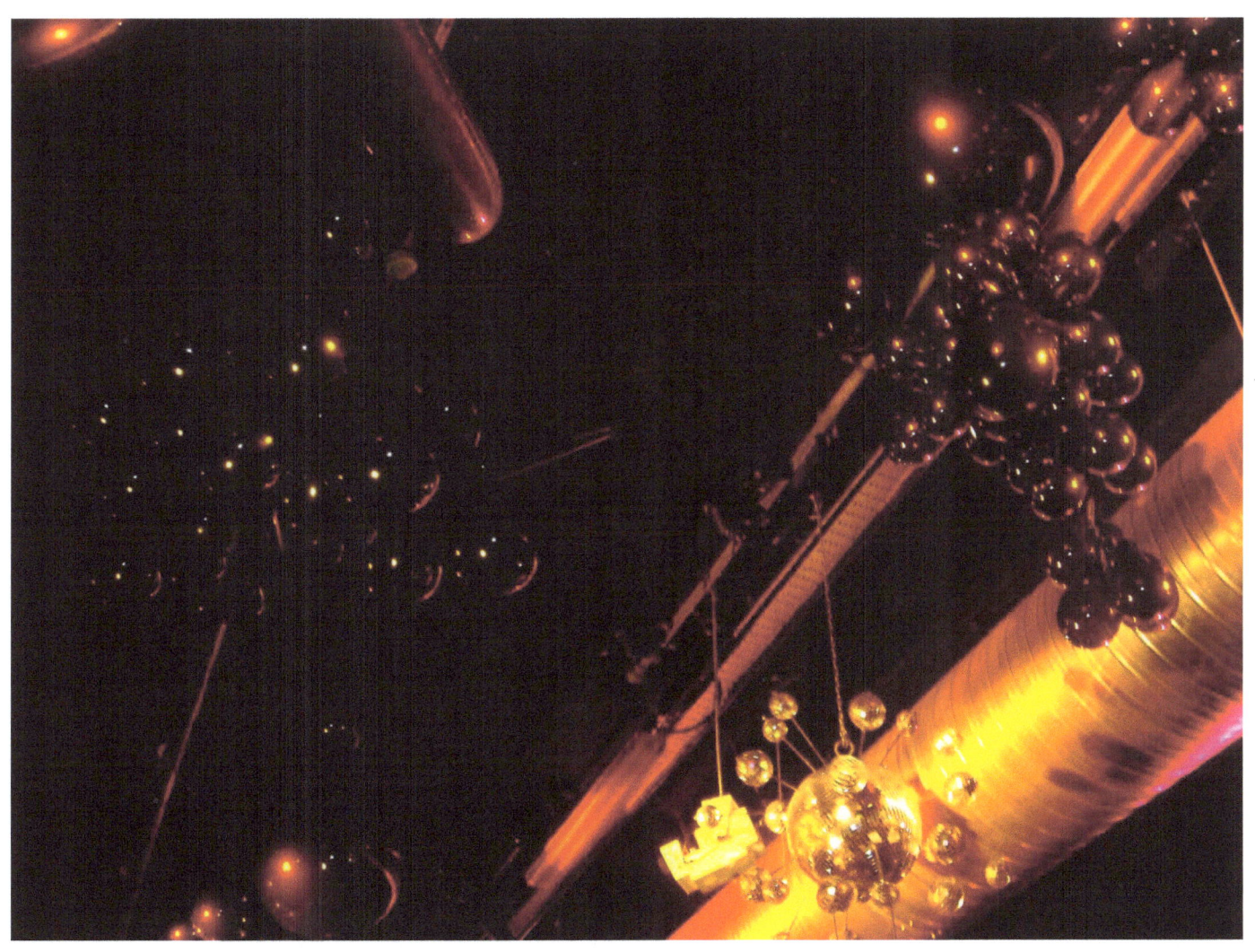

Used helium and floated the forms. The room was all black and they looked like glass. The vibrated and to the sounds from the band in the back room and people discovered this and hugged the ones they could touch. I left around 2 in the morning.

Southern California

Riverside Art Museum, 2006

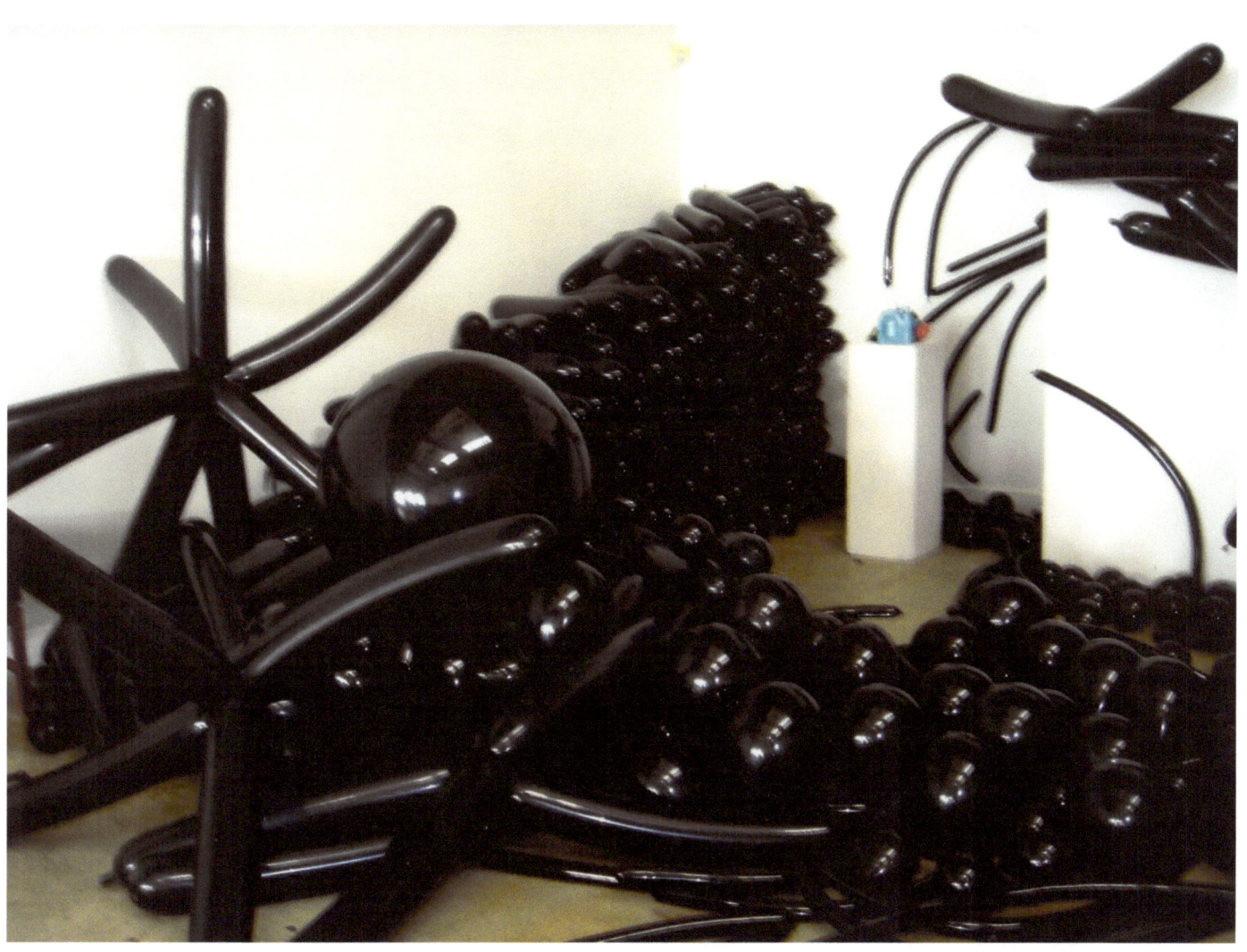

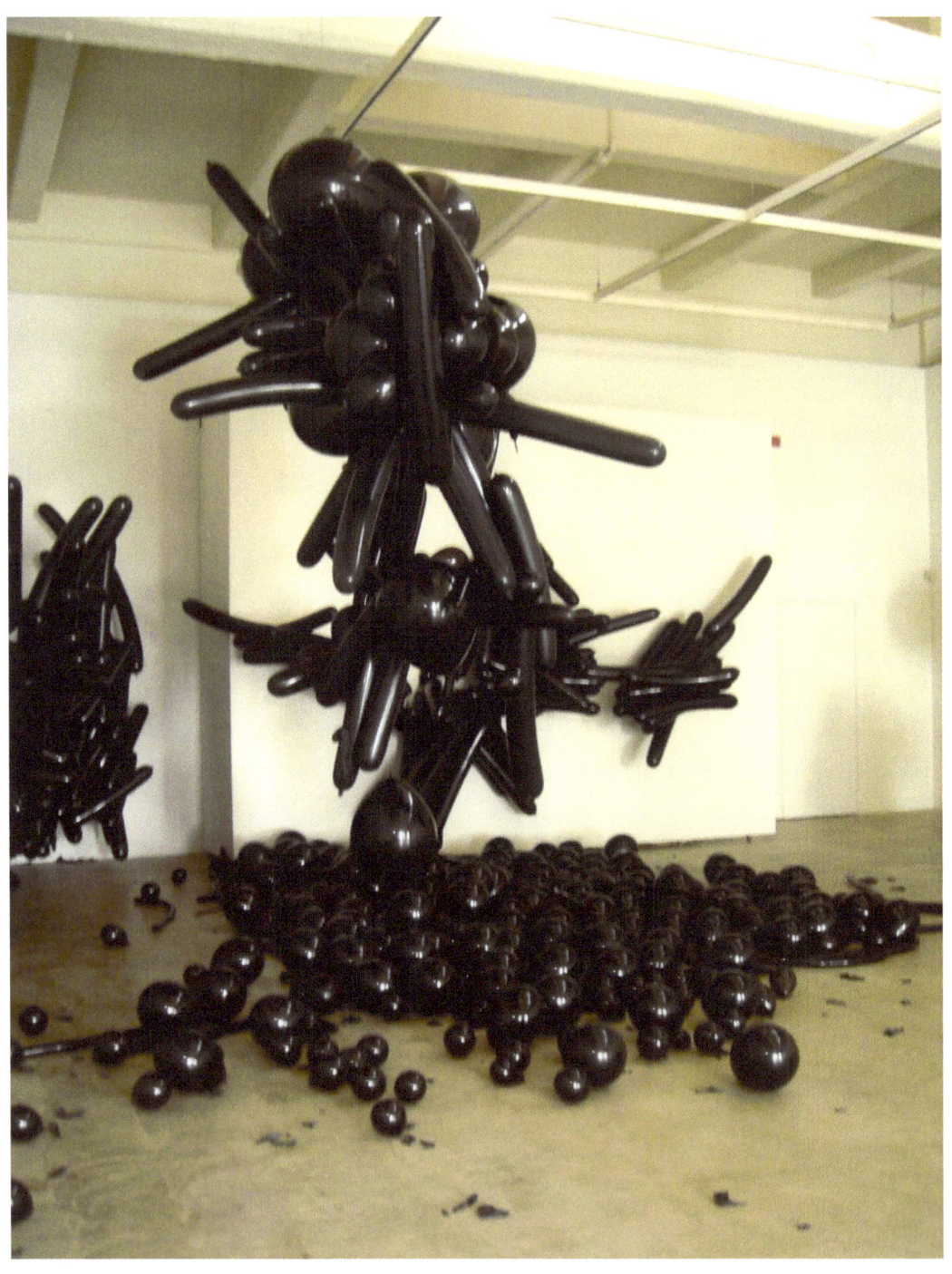

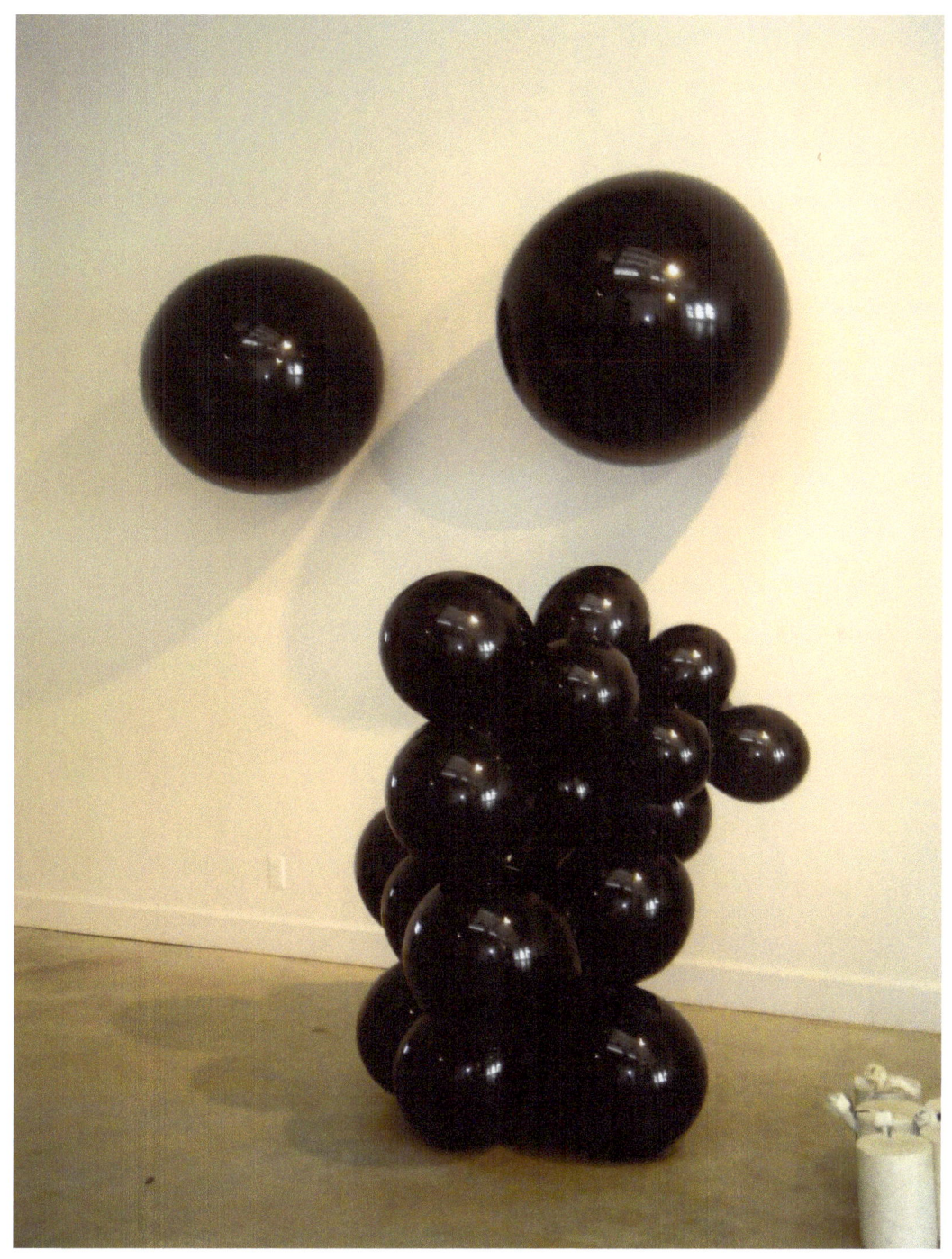

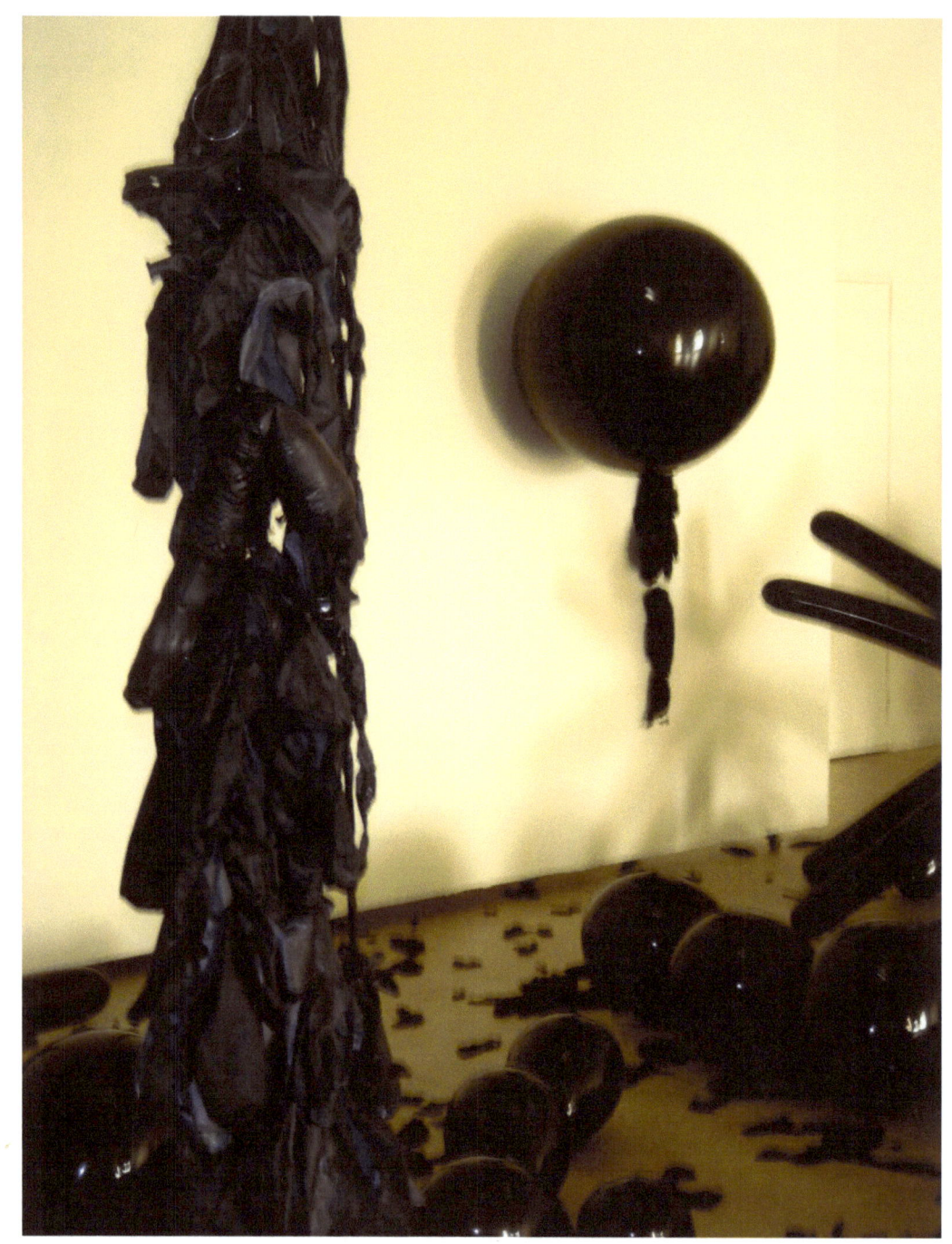

New York City

The Lab, 2007

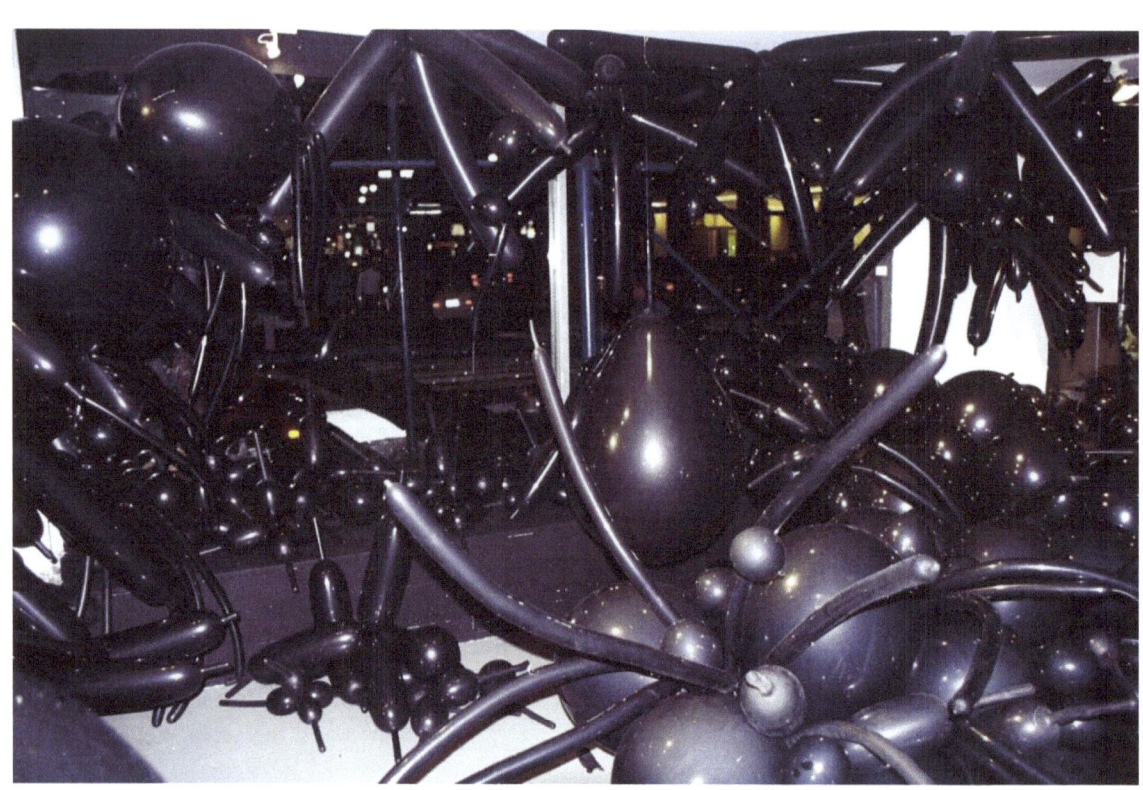

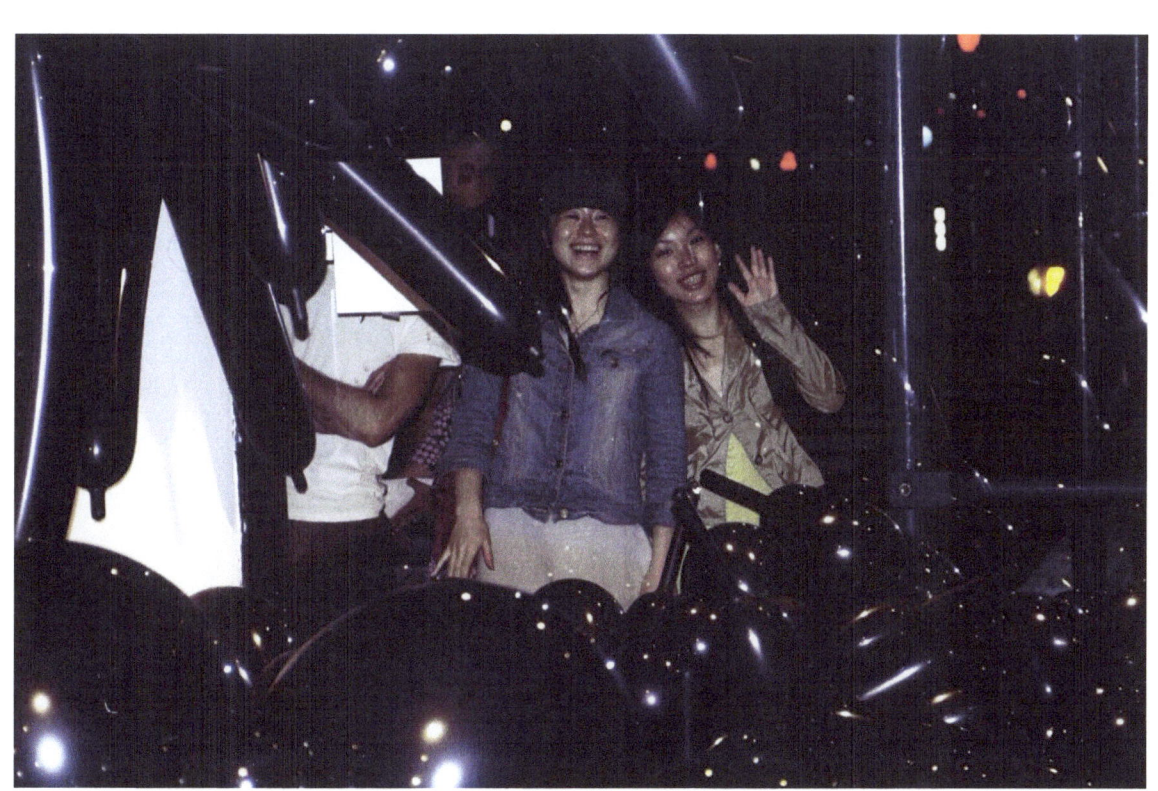

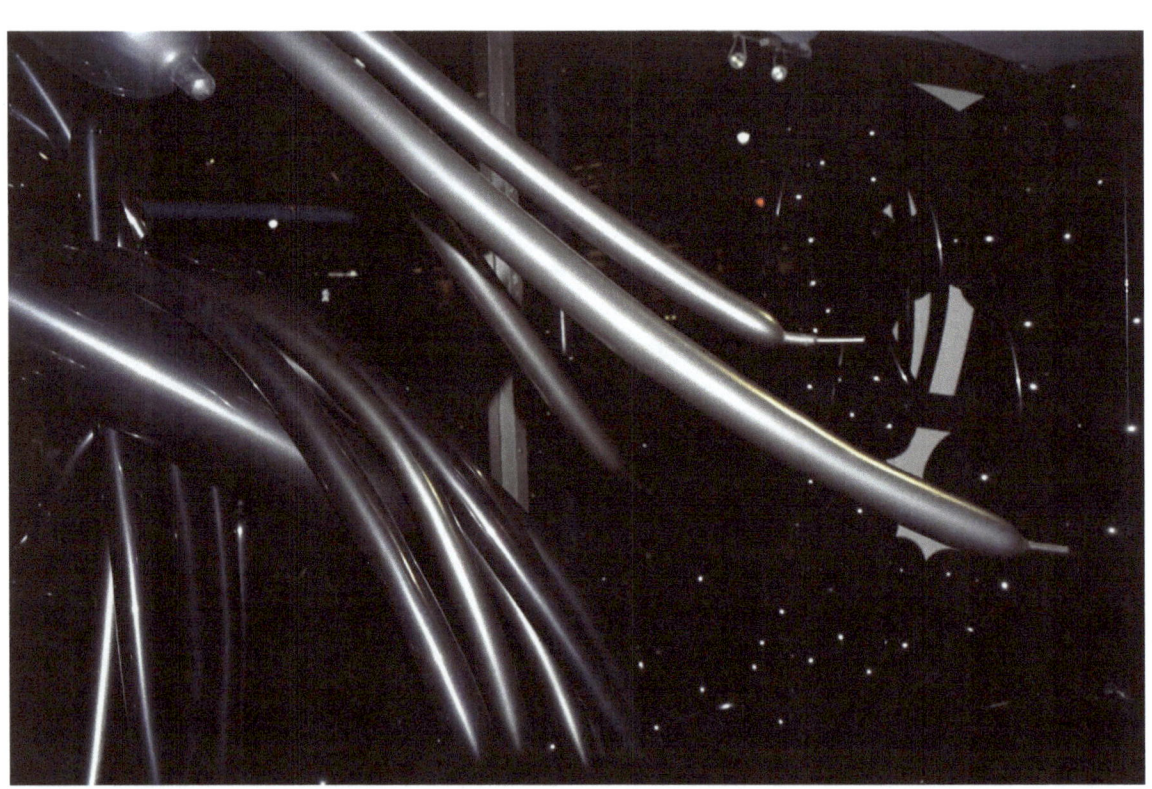

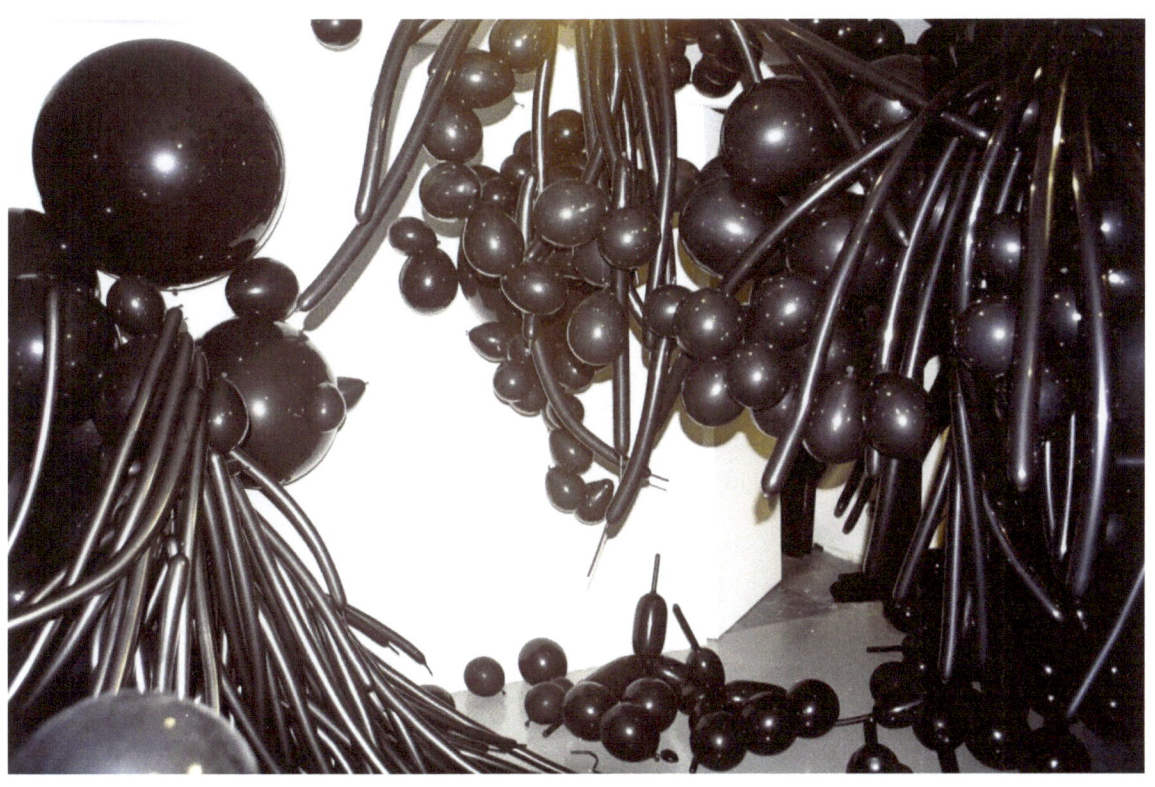

Video of the pop: http://www.youtube.com/watch?v=cyuLnX6YRaA

Puerto Varas, Chile

Galería y Centro Cultural Bosque Nativo, 2012

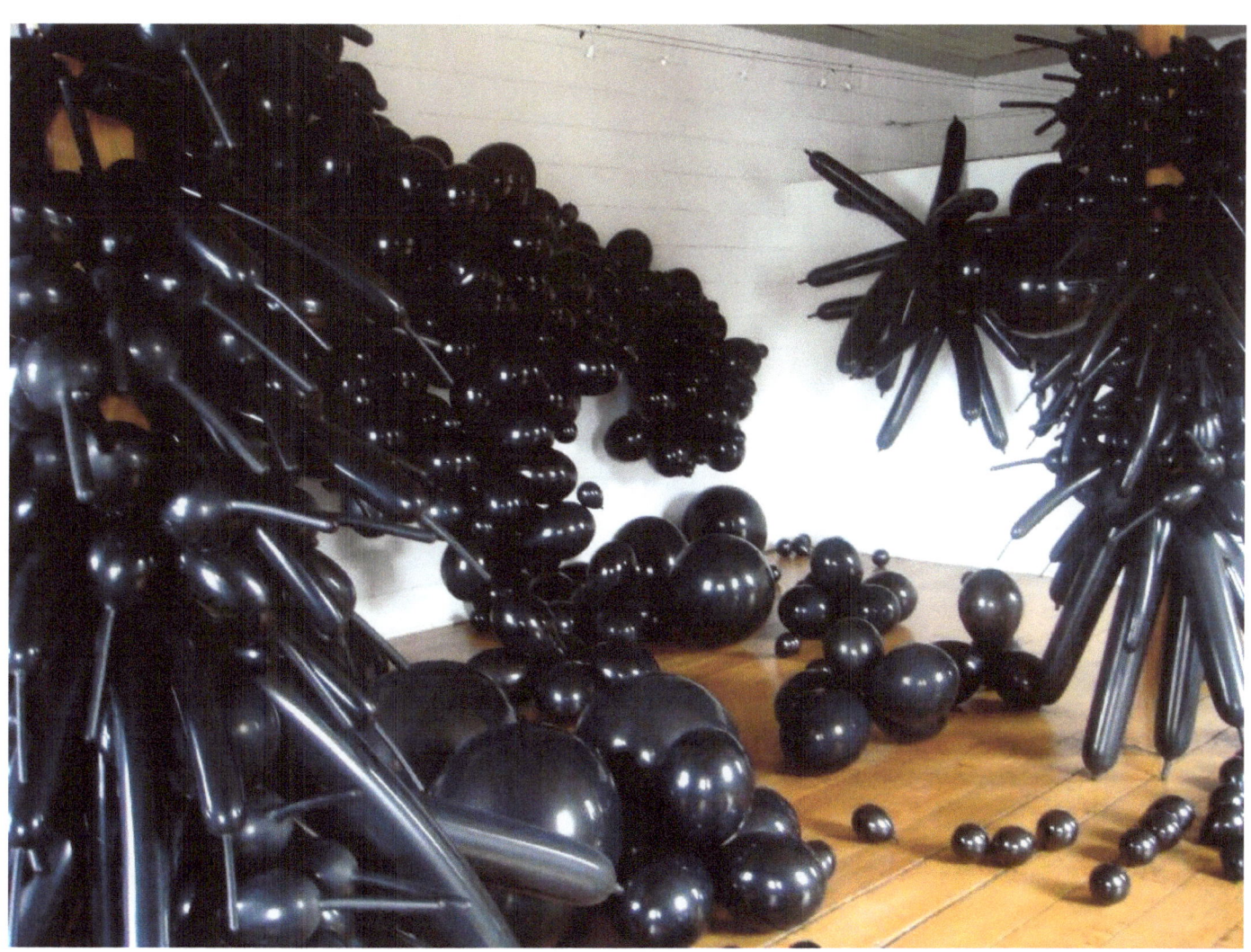

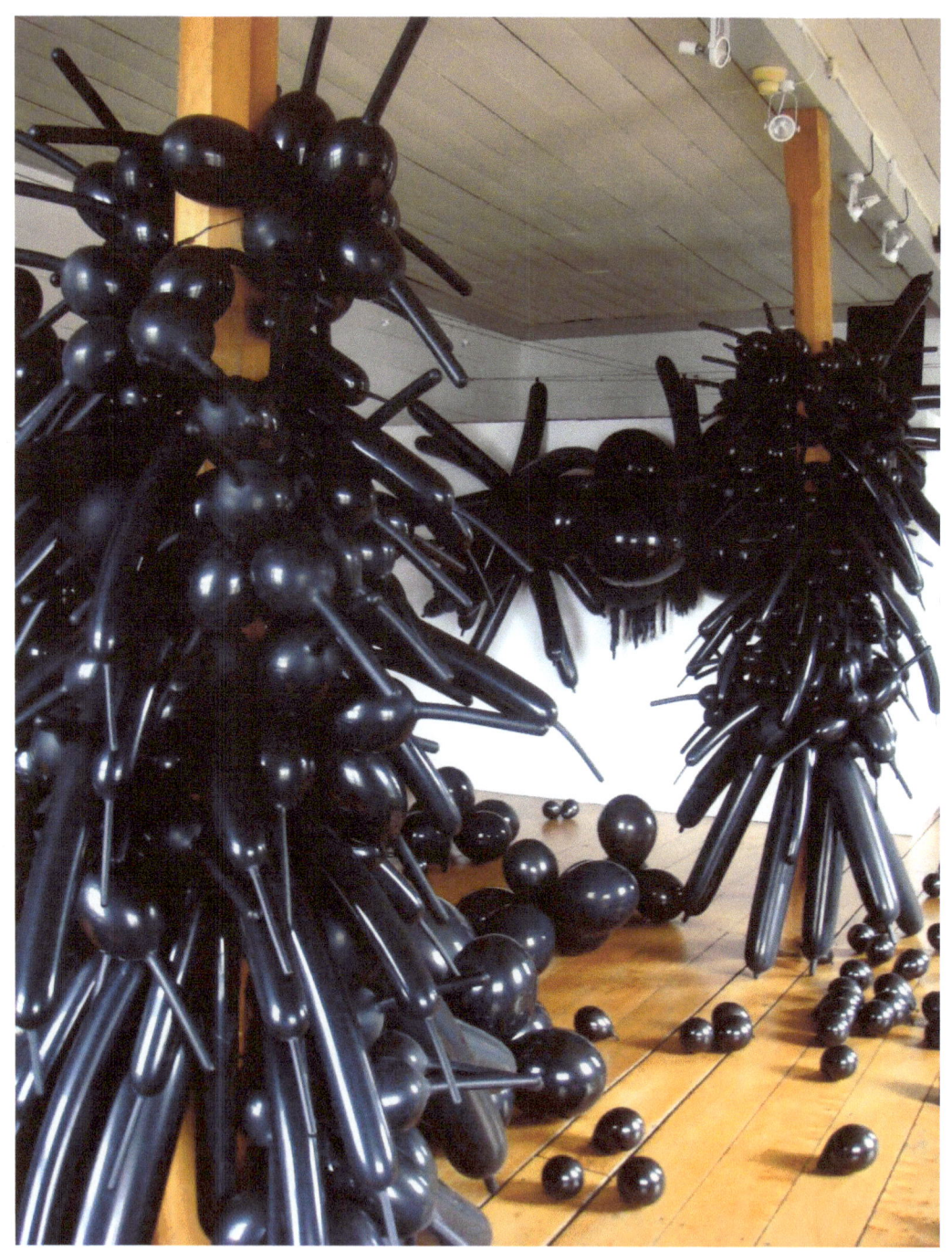

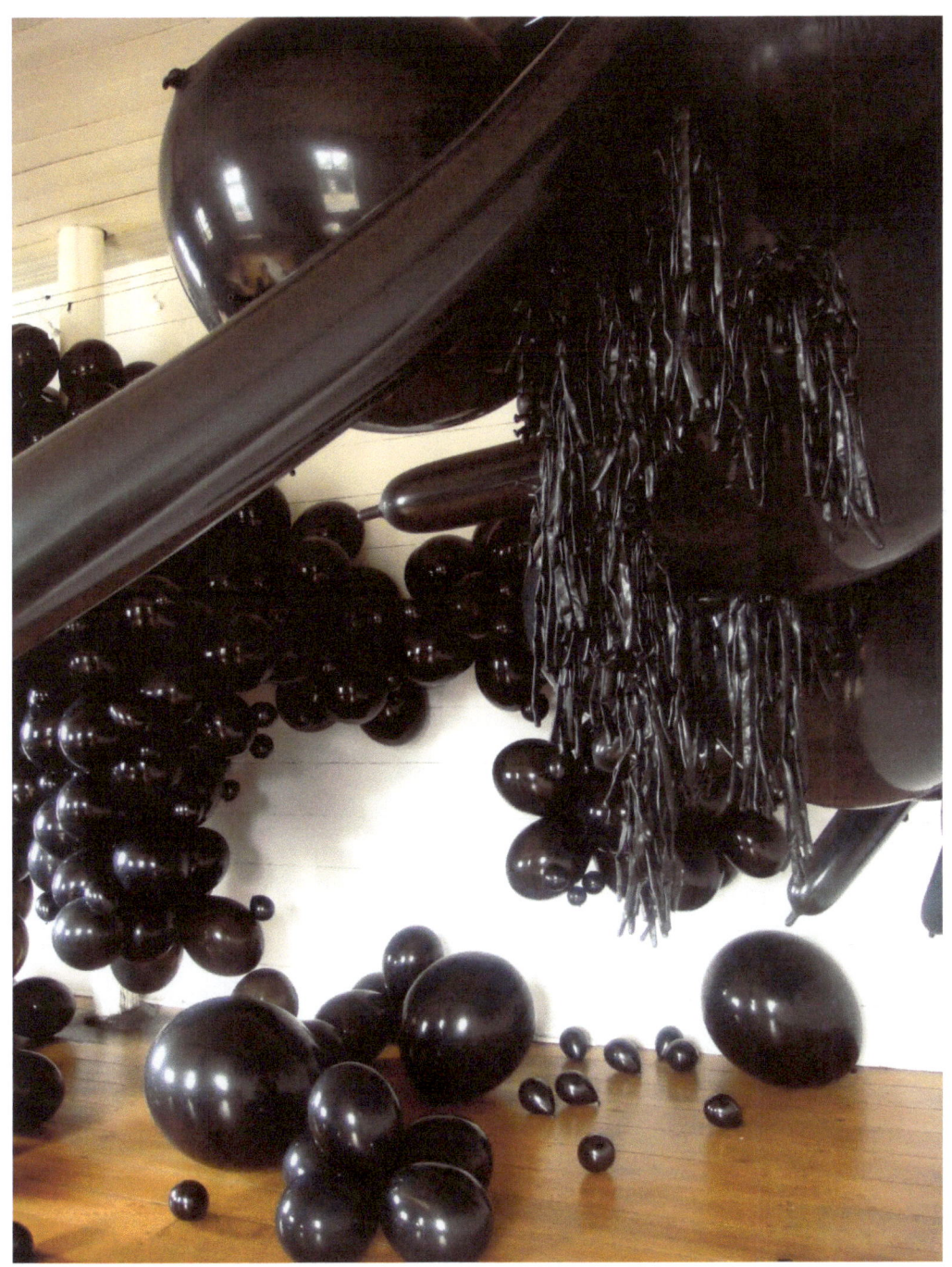

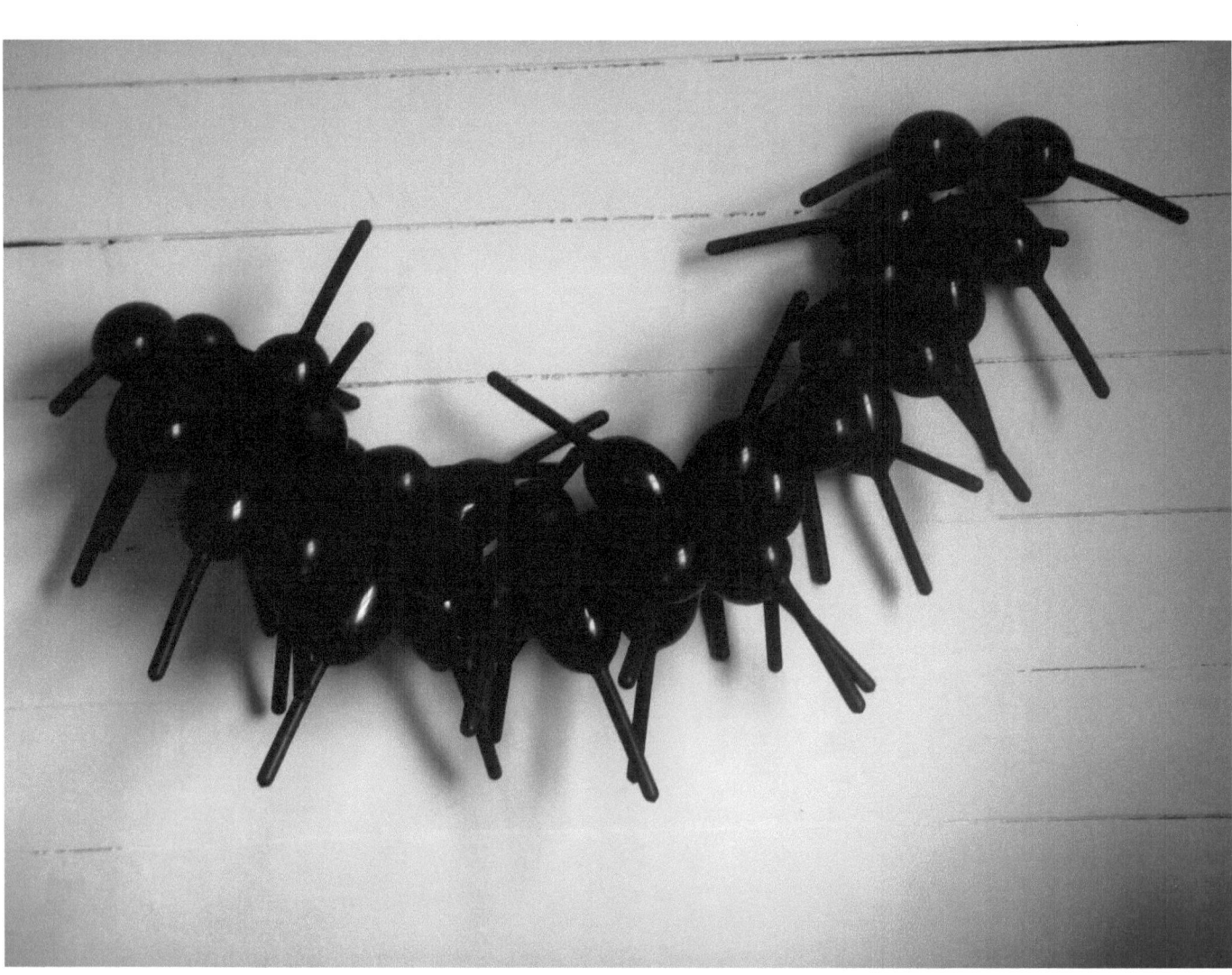

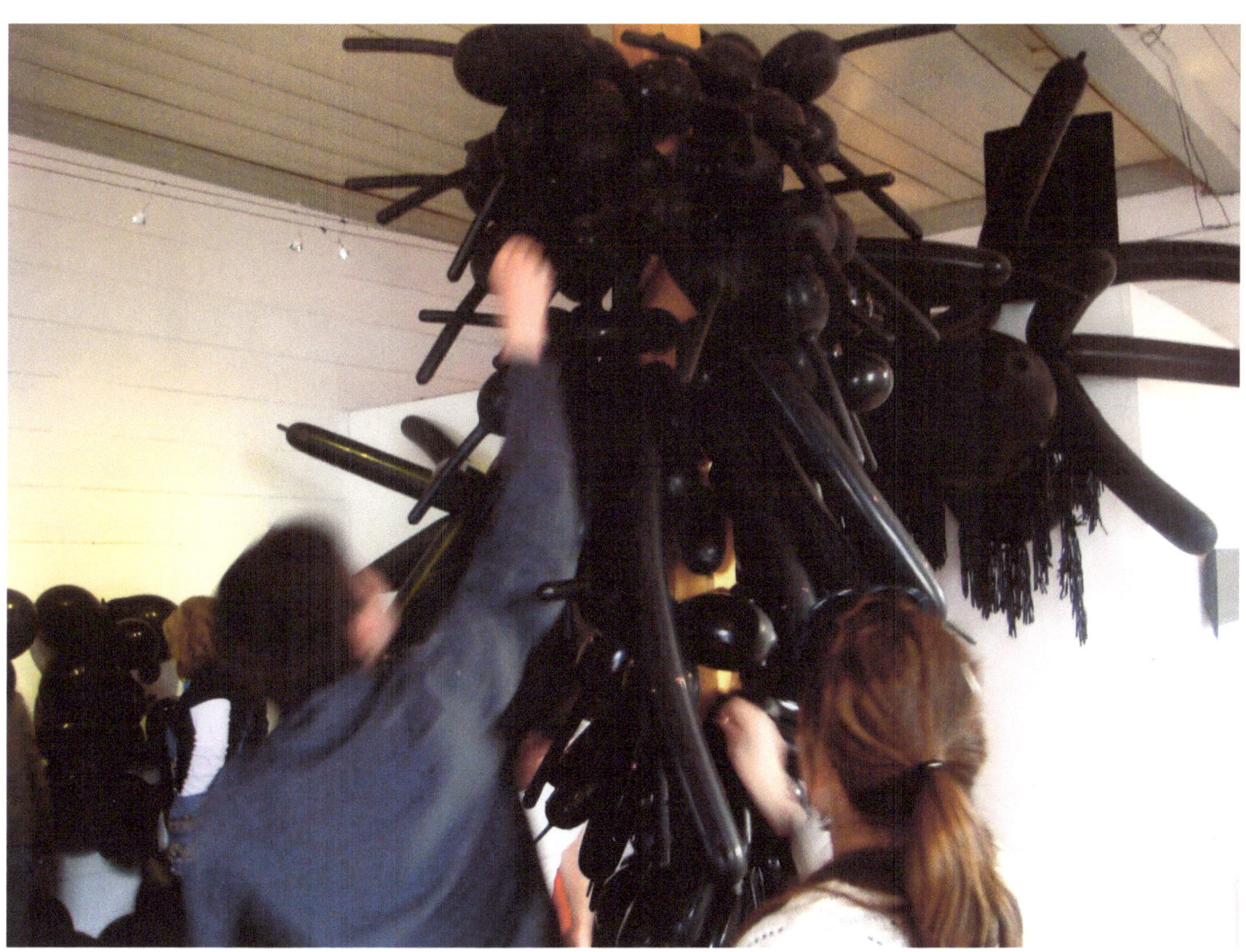

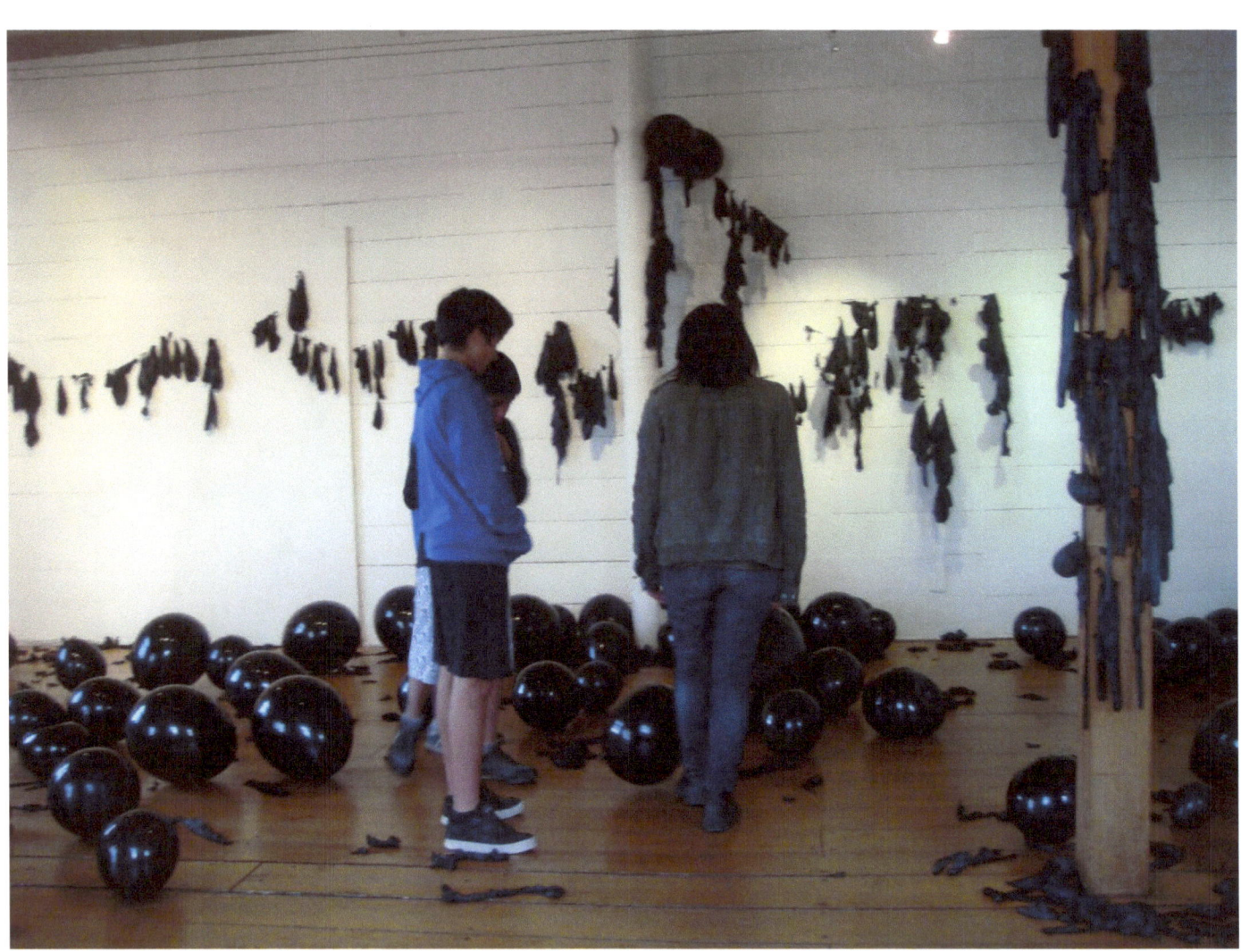

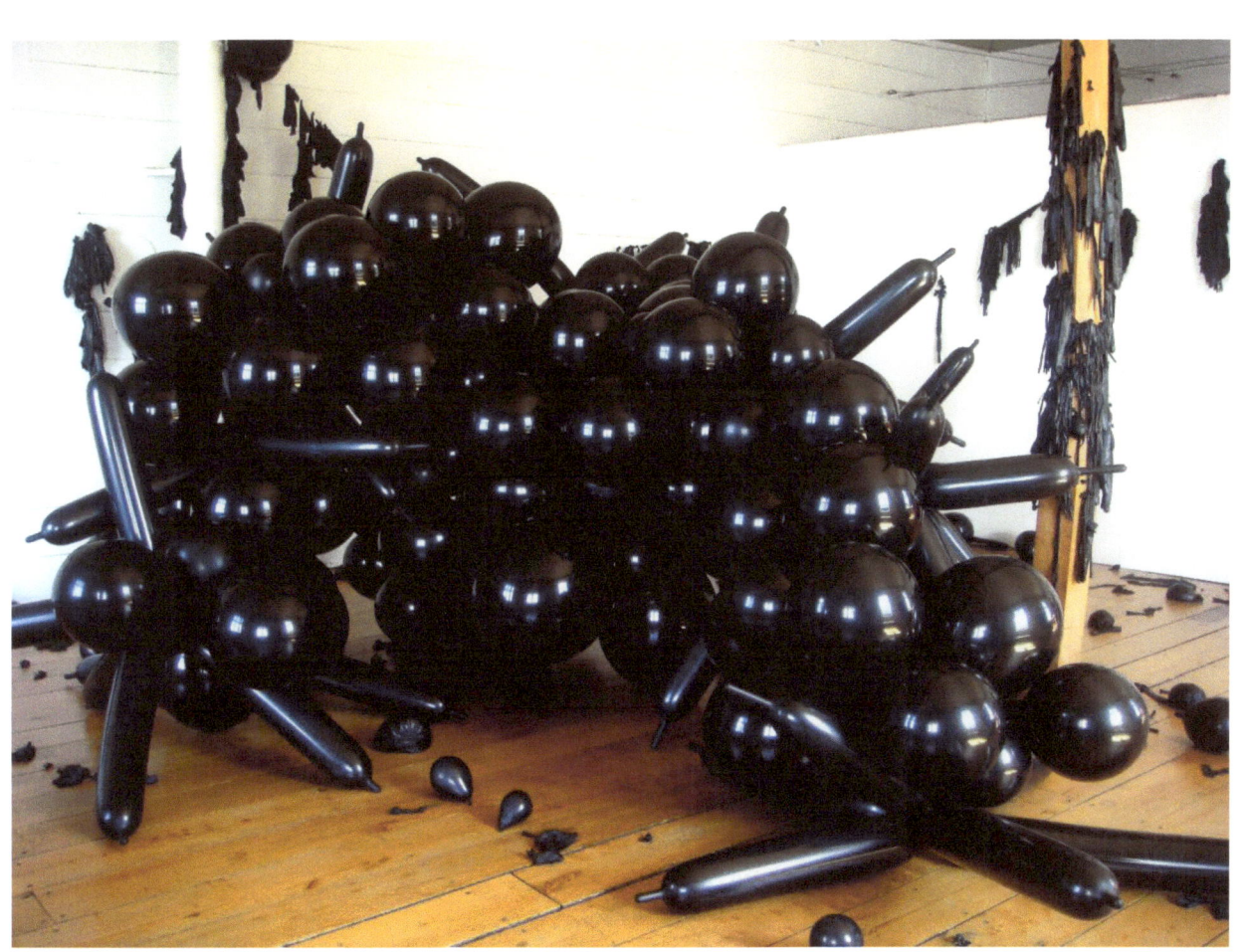